Coping with Infuriating, Mean, Critical People

Coping with Infuriating, Mean, Critical People

The Destructive Narcissistic Pattern

NINA W. BROWN

PRAEGER

Westport, Connecticut
London

Library of Congress Cataloging-in-Publication Data

Brown, Nina W.
    Coping with infuriating, mean, critical people : the destructive narcissistic
    pattern / Nina W. Brown.
       p.   cm.
    Includes bibliographical references and index.
    ISBN 0–275–98984–4 (alk. paper)
    1. Narcissism.   I. Title.
  BF575.N35B75   2006
  158.2—dc22   2006021042

British Library Cataloguing in Publication Data is available.

Library of Congress Catalog Card Number: 2006021042
ISBN: 0–275–98984–4

First published in 2006

Praeger Publishers, 88 Post Road West, Westport, CT 06881
An imprint of Greenwood Publishing Group, Inc.
www.praeger.com

Printed in the United States of America

The paper used in this book complies with the
Permanent Paper Standard issued by the National
Information Standards Organization (Z39.48–1984).

10 9 8 7 6 5 4 3 2 1

This book is dedicated to my husband
Wil

my children
Toni, Mike, and Linda

and my grandchildren
Billy, Joey, Samantha, Christopher, Nicholas, and Emma.

Contents

Preface

The feedback received from readers of my earlier book, *The Destructive Narcissistic Pattern* (1998), encouraged this new publication. The behaviors and attitudes described were familiar to many who met the description for a DNP. It was interesting to note from the readers' communications that the strong and negative feelings aroused by that person either endured over time, or were easily recalled with no lessening of intensity. This observation provided me with the major emphasis and focus for this book, that of trying to guide readers in understanding why they react as they do, and why it can be difficult to let go of those intense and negative feelings. Having been through a similar experience gave me a deeper understanding of the difficulties, but the experience also encouraged my research and creation of effective strategies that I could use to help myself. These strategies worked for me and I pass them on to you with the caveat that you are different from me, and that what worked for me may not fit your personality. However, reading about some strategies can encourage and trigger your personal creative strategies to fit your personality and your situation.

Other intents for this book are that you, the reader, gain some new awareness and understanding about your self, your possible undeveloped narcissism, and how you are causing your own reactions. It will be most helpful for you to build your self, so that the negative feelings you experience in and after interactions with a destructive narcissist are either not triggered, or are much less intense and do not endure. Since you, or anyone else, are powerless to change the destructive narcissist, it becomes empowering to realize that there are actions you can take that will help to reduce or eliminate negative effects on you.

I am often asked if people with a DNP will or can ever change. My answer is that yes, they can change, but only when they want to change. Change cannot be imposed externally in these cases. On the other hand, many of these people do not see a need to change as it is their perception that they are fine; it's you who has a problem. I hope that what is written here will be helpful to you.

Nina W. Brown

CHAPTER 1

Who Are These Infuriating and Difficult People?

EXAMPLE 1

Eric is an administrator at a college where he is on the faculty. He sought for years to become an administrator and tended to associate only with those who had administrative positions. While Eric had received several administrative assignments through the years, he had not received an assignment that had a budget line, personnel, and other resources that indicate some measure of power and status. He did not fail to point out how much better qualified he was than others who received such assignments and continued to lobby for an administrative position, which was finally awarded to him.

Eric was married and divorced four times, and each divorce was filled with strife and acrimony. He is quick to tell everyone how inadequate, crazy, and wrong his ex-wives are. He was recently married, but his new wife developed serious medical problems that constrain activities, such as travel. He made statements about the constraints that invited, or seemed to require, expressions of sympathy from others.

Almost immediately after receiving the administrative position, Eric managed to get into arguments with almost every faculty member in his unit. He was so demanding—sometimes unreasonably so—blaming and critical that he lost three secretaries in the space of two years. Faculty and staff found it very frustrating to try to talk with him about practically everything, as every conversation resulted in his criticizing, blaming, and belittling the person.

Eric was also very much a micromanager. He insisted that office supplies, such as paper clips, be reluctantly doled out, but only after the person had made a good case for why they should have some. Pointing out to him how demeaning this was only resulted in more blame and criticism about everything concerning the person who spoke up, not just the topic under discussion.

He also lied, made misleading and distorted statements, and tried to get faculty and staff to criticize each other. If confronted with the falsehood or error, he was very adept at turning it back on the speaker. He would never admit being in error about anything, and when his lies were revealed, he tossed it off by saying that the other person misunderstood or was deliberately lying to make him, Eric, look bad.

One of the most troubling behaviors was his habit of giving orders to faculty. In an academic setting, faculty are accustomed to being treated as peers. When there is a task to be done, one or more faculty are asked or assigned to do it, and in 99.9 percent of the cases, they accept responsibility for the task. Everyone understands that there are shared responsibilities and that everyone is expected to contribute. Eric, on the other hand, felt that his position entitled him to order faculty to do something and that they should promptly obey. He would not ask someone to do a task; he would tell them that they were to do it, and the order was followed by a memo thanking them for volunteering. This resulted in many feelings of resentment. Faculty and staff also found it very frustrating to try to resolve conflicts with Eric. Whenever any conversation was initiated to present him with the other person's perspective and to make it clear that the person would like to work out any differences, his response was such that invariably the other person left feeling more frustrated, angry, and upset than when they started.

Eric's story illustrates many of the situations, behaviors, and attitudes that make it difficult to understand that you may be dealing with a destructive narcissist.

- Many failed and unsatisfying relationships.
- Comments about others that are blaming, criticizing, demeaning, and devaluing.
- Constant references to his superiority.
- Lies, distortions, and misleading statements.
- Interactions that frequently produced resentment, anger, and other negative intense feelings for others.
- Never admitting making mistakes.

These are examples to illustrate the troubling behaviors and attitudes; and because these can be difficult to describe, and the distressing events unfolded over time, and attempts to understand and to resolve differences did not succeed, it is understandable that you stay in a state of turmoil and do not understand that person or your reactions.

Narcissism is generally thought to be an excessive focus or love of one's self, and is used as a label that is not complementary. When someone is termed a narcissist, it usually conveys something very negative about that person. The psychological theory of self-psychology uses the term somewhat differently, and that is the perspective used in this book. The term used here thinks of narcissism as self-love, but not excessive or negative. Indeed, some love of self is the foundation for self-esteem, self-confidence, and self-efficacy. This perspective also allows narcissism to be dynamic, capable of development and growth, and as having a healthy aspect. Readers will be presented with information to help them understand

- age-appropriate narcissism
- healthy adult narcissism
- behaviors and attitudes reflective of undeveloped narcissism
- what constitutes a Destructive Narcissistic Pattern (DNP)

Have you encountered anyone whose behavior and/or attitudes are similar to the following:

- Constantly makes comments to or about you that are devaluing or demeaning.
- Interactions with this person generally leave you angry, upset, hurt, or resentful.
- You, and others, seemingly have to give their desires, wishes, and needs a lot of attention, care, and priority.
- The relationship began on a high note, you were charmed, but now cannot do anything to please him or her no matter how hard you try.
- The person cannot be trusted to give accurate information, and frequently lies, distorts, and misleads.
- Demands understanding from you, but gives none in return.
- Every conversation somehow gets focused on him or her.
- Uses or takes your possessions without permission and/or fails to return them.

These are just a few of the behaviors and attitudes that suggest that the person may have a Destructive Narcissistic Pattern (DNP). No one behavior or attitude defines this pattern; it is a group of these that define it.

The label "destructive narcissist" was developed as a description for someone who consistently exhibits numerous and intense characteristics usually associated with the pathological narcissist, but has fewer of these character-istics, and some of these may be less intense. The term is intended to give structure to behaviors, attitudes, and feelings displayed by some with whom you live, work, love, and interact on a regular basis who consistently pro-duce feelings of incompetence, inadequacy, and frustration in you as well as other uncomfortable feelings in others. These troubling behaviors and atti-tudes make interactions and relationships difficult, leave you and others with distressing feelings, and are marked by a noticeable lack of empathy termed the destructive narcissistic pattern (DNP).

The focus for this book is adult destructive narcissism that has roots in the person's parental and family of origin relationships that impacted and influenced the developing self. This approach provides some understanding of how the self develops. Also discussed are possible strategies for helping you build, fortify, and develop yourself, and this further developed self can help you better deal with people who demonstrate a DNP.

Narcissism can be thought of as a continuum ranging from healthy at one end to pathological at the other. Healthy narcissism in adults is characterized by creativity, empathy, an appropriate sense of humor, awareness of finiteness, responsibility, self-reflection, and wisdom. Age-appropriate healthy adult nar-cissism is also viewed as the ability to experience a healthy appreciation and enjoyment of your activities, a sense of direction, and a system of values that guides you together with a helpful feeling of disappointment that incorpo-rates some nondebilitating anger and shame when you fail to live up to your expectations of yourself. Let's begin with the story of Narcissus from which the original term and description was derived.

FICTIONAL AND REAL NARCISSISM

The story of Narcissus has been used by many as descriptive of narcissism, especially pathological narcissism. Narcissus, in Greek mythology, was a young man of exceptional physical beauty. All of the nymphs desired him, but he showed no interest in any of them. A nymph named Echo loved him deeply and approached him one day to tell him of her love for him. Narcissus rudely rejected her, and feeling very shamed and grieving, she faded away until only her voice was left.

The nymphs were outraged and petitioned the gods to punish Narcissus. The gods granted the nymphs' wish for vengeance by setting the stage for Narcissus to experience unrequited love as did Echo. Narcissus saw his own image, which he thought was a beautiful water spirit, in a clear mountain pool one day and immediately fell in love. The reflection, of course, did not respond and disappeared every time he tried to embrace it. Narcissus, who continued to try to get a response, was unable to tear himself away from the reflection. This went on for some time, and Narcissus gradually pined away and died. When the nymphs came to bury him, they found in his place a flower facing the water.

This short tale contains many of the concepts associated with narcissism, especially destructive narcissism. Characteristics such as self-centeredness, lack of empathy, shallow emotional life, arrogance, need for admiration by others, and an inability to form and maintain satisfying relationships are associated with destructive narcissism. Following is another description of a destructive narcissist.

EXAMPLE 2

Helen is in her third marriage, and the other two ended in divorce. Both the second and third husbands were married when they met her, and both divorced their wives to marry her. Helen now works in a setting that includes her first husband's second wife, her second husband and his first wife, and her third husband.

Helen has ordered her personal and professional activities around associating with powerful people. She name-drops, belongs to the same organizations as the socially powerful and prominent, and makes sure she attends the same events. She pushed her second husband to buy a summer home in the place where many of the desirable power people had summer homes and made sure her coworkers knew that she had the house and frequently associated with these people.

Helen is very adept at making some people feel she finds them exciting and interesting, especially new acquaintances. She is solicitous, complimentary, and asks their opinions often. However, if the acquaintances remain in the vicinity for a while, she pays them little attention and may even ignore them. Sometimes she makes cutting remarks, criticizes them openly, or devalues their input. These people often seem bewildered at the turn of events.

One of her most troubling characteristics is her hypersensitivity to what she perceives as critical of her. It does not matter that the person intended no criticism nor that no one else who heard the remark thought it was critical, she reacts as if the person deliberately sought to hurt her. No amount of explanation makes any difference, and many people often find themselves apologizing to her and feeling put upon or stupid for having to do so.

What behaviors and attitudes suggest that Helen has a DNP?

- Many failed intimate relationships
- Concern for power and status, and spending considerable money to associate with people thought to have these
- Critical, demeaning, and devaluing of others
- Hypersensitive to perceived criticism

The discussions in the book have two goals: to better understand and cope with others who have some destructive narcissistic characteristics, and to increase awareness of personal destructive narcissistic behaviors, attitudes, and feelings. The first goal is addressed by presenting descriptions of the defining pattern of behaviors and attitudes that are so troubling to most people who interact with them on a regular basis. The second goal is addressed by frequently reminding you to examine your thoughts, feelings, behaviors, and attitudes as these may be having unintended effects, and your awareness need to be increased. It is also possible that you are in some measure, contributing to your own distress, and this is something you can change.

DOES SOMEONE IN YOUR LIFE HAVE A DNP?

Is there someone in your life with whom you interact on a regular basis that routinely makes you feel frustrated, angry, inadequate, and/or incompetent?

1. Is this person unique in provoking these feelings?
2. Do many other people have this effect on you?
3. Do most others who interact with this person on a routine basis report having these same feelings?
4. Are you the only one who has these reactions?

The following survey is designed to help determine whether the individual you had in mind when you answered the four items above could be thought of as having a DNP. The survey asks you to rate your perceptions of this person's attitudes and behaviors based on your interactions with him or her.

PERCEPTION OF ATTITUDES AND BEHAVIOR

DIRECTIONS: Think of someone in a current relationship that you find difficult. The difficulty can be in the relationship, understanding him or her, communicating effectively with him or her, or other behaviors. As you read the items, try to rate them using the following scale.

5 – almost always	4 – usually	3 – sometimes
2 – occasionally	1 – almost never	

In my interactions with the person I would describe him or her as

1. Needing to be the center of attention.
2. Competing for attention.
3. Fishing for flattery, external validation, and approval.
4. Engaging in one-upmanship.
5. Seeking favors but not returning them.
6. Insensitive and indifferent to others' concerns.
7. Knowing what's best for others and is not reluctant in telling others what to do and feel.
8. Having contempt for others who are not as accomplished, successful, handsome, and so on.
9. Having the correct words for feelings, but not conveying the genuine feeling behind the words.
10. Having an unrealistic perception of personal competencies, and can take on too many tasks.
11. Expecting others to cater to his or her demands or desires.
12. Expecting others to read his or her mind and fulfill needs, desires, and wishes.
13. Having an attitude that others should subjugate their needs for them.
14. Feeling free to make cutting, sarcastic, demeaning, or devaluing remarks to and about others.
15. Easily offended by others' comments, taking them personally, and not accepting that the comments are not attacks.
16. Someone who lies, distorts, and misleads.
17. Perceiving everything and everyone in terms of self.
18. Overcontrolling, blaming others for their mistakes, and overly critical of others.

19. Unable to be pleased by anyone or anything.

20. Mistrustful, resentful, and envious.

SCORING: Add the numbers you checked to obtain a total score.

Total Score Descriptions

80–100: This individual provokes most of the intense reactions generally felt by many who interact with him or her on a regular basis. Before terming the individual you rated as having a DNP, your ratings of interactions with him or her must be confirmed by others who interact with the person on a regular basis. If your ratings are not confirmed or only partially confirmed, then it may be helpful to consider whether you may be overreacting to perceived criticism or disapproval from them.

60–79: Scores in this range are suggestive of the DNP. The reactions are less intense than in the category just given but differ only in their intensity. As with the other category, your reactions need to be confirmed by the experiences of others who interact with this individual very frequently. If confirmed, the individual is exhibiting many of the traits and characteristics associated with the DNP. If not confirmed, your reactions are personal and should be explored as such.

40–59: This range of scores defines an individual who is exhibiting some DNP traits and characteristics that are troubling to others who interact with him or her on a regular basis. The behavior is inconsistent but occurs often enough to provoke negative feelings and frustration in others. These ratings of reactions also need to be confirmed by others to reduce or eliminate the possibility that these are your personal reactions not induced by the rated individual's behavior.

20–39: If the scores fall into this range, the rated individual is exhibiting few of the troubling or DNP traits and characteristics, and those that are exhibited are exhibited inconsistently.

Below 20: This score indicates little or no troubling DNP traits or characteristics.

Descriptions for Behaviors and Attitudes on the Scale

After rating the individual read the following descriptions for scale items and see if you would change any of the ratings you gave. Completing the scale before reading descriptions allows you to know what your immediate reactions and perceptions are about this individual. Reflection can help you eliminate possible personal bias or confirm your previous ratings. Each of the behaviors, attitudes, and feelings is briefly discussed.

Center of attention. It does not matter what the event or situation is; this person finds some way to focus attention on him or herself. Examples are a raised voice, starting an argument, acting inappropriately for the occasion, dressing to be outrageous, interrupting, and other such acts.

Competing for attention. You only have to remember or think of sibling rivalry to understand how competition takes place. All competition is not direct, open, or visible, and immediately identifiable. Sometimes there is misbehavior, an event exaggerated to become a crisis, an imagined worry, and so on. Whatever the person can do to receive the desired attention is considered to be fair game in the competition.

Fishing for flattery and so on. This need can be somewhat disguised as when someone asks your opinion, but really wants your approval or to be flattered. It can also be more visible as when someone brings up a personal accomplishment and others are expected to be admiring.

One-upmanship. Bigger, better, more, and greater are the usual concepts for one-upmanship. Whatever someone does, has, accomplishes, and so on, is topped. This also extends to adversity, troubles, and tragedy. Their experiences were worse, had greater constraints, were more troubling, and so on.

Seeking favors but no reciprocity. This person frequently seeks favors from others, but there is usually some reason why the favor cannot be returned. This is also the person who "borrows" others' possessions without first asking permission, does not return what was borrowed in a reasonable time or ever, and can act offended when you ask for your possession to be returned.

Insensitive and indifferent. An illustration would be when a spouse describes an unsettling and upsetting experience, the other spouse says a few words acknowledging that the other was heard, and then asks what's for dinner. Yes, this person hears the words but is insensitive and indifferent to the other spouse's concern.

Knowing what's best for others. This occurs when you are not expected or allowed to have thoughts or feelings that are different from the other person. The boss who ignores or rejects ideas from others, parents who expect their children to think like them, or spouses who speak for the other are some examples. Ideas and opinions from others are discouraged. Any resources that may be available are not freely given or access to them is not provided; instead, they are carefully monitored and doled out as if you are receiving a special gift and have little or no right to it.

If you should be so bold as to express a differing thought or feeling, propose an idea, or have an opinion, it will be disparaged and criticized. However, be aware that you will meet your thought, idea, or opinion again, but it will then be the destructive narcissist's idea or opinion.

Closely related to all of the preceding items is always knowing what is best for others and what should or should not be done. There are those who by their experience, knowledge, and wisdom can know what is "best" some of the time, but no one knows what is best for everyone all of the time. A destructive narcissist who has this characteristic is very willing to let you know what you should and ought to do without your having to ask.

Contempt for others. Confidence in self and one's abilities is developed through interactions with others who are supportive even when mistakes are made. Confidence is eroded and undermined when you and/or your work are constantly devalued. Such devaluation is also on a more personal level than criticism of your work; it is a put-down of you as a person. You are made to feel incapable, incompetent, and stupid. Children need to develop confidence in themselves for healthy growth and development. Adults need to maintain their confidence, and this is very difficult to do if there is constant devaluing of you and your input.

Nothing behind the words. This is difficult to describe or illustrate, but if you have ever experienced someone who did not mean what he or she said, then you understand what is meant by having the words, but not the feelings. Listening only to words helps you miss much of the message, and can lead you to misjudging the person.

Unrealistic perception of competencies. Trying something new and/or difficult is to be encouraged and commended. However, there should be a realistic appraisal of your competencies, knowledge, and abilities before attempting this as you don't set out to fail. On the other hand, when someone has an unrealistic perception about him or herself, it is easy to become overwhelmed, and to fail to live up to expectations.

Catering to him or her. Parents who expect their children to drop what they are doing to take care of the parent's demands or wishes are one example. Lovers and spouses who expect that the other's attention and priorities are on them is another example. Bosses and colleagues who expect you to do what they want when they want it are other examples.

Mindreading. This is the expectation that others should or ought to know what is needed or desired, and give it to the person without that person having to verbalize the need or desire. Have you ever experienced someone saying to you that you should or ought to know what he or she means, wants, or needs without being told? This can be extremely frustrating to the receiver, and induce shame for not being good enough to read that person's mind.

Subjugating needs. In deep, satisfying, and meaningful relationships there is usually collaboration about whose needs receive priority at any given time, except in the cases of children, the elderly, or illness. The person who has this attitude does not fit that description, but conveys the thought that others' needs are not as important or pressing, and that his or her needs should and must receive priority all, or most, of the time.

Unpleasant remarks. Although professed to be teasing, playing, or joking, when someone makes cutting, demeaning, devaluing, and sarcastic remarks, these are unpleasant for the receiver. There is an undercurrent of attacking, contempt, and or arrogance by the speaker who is seeking to elevate him or herself by negative remarks about others.

Overreacting to perceived criticism. Few, if any, people like to be criticized. Most of us are able to accept criticism without feeling personally attacked. Being overreactive to perceived criticism means that the person feels attacked on a very personal level and fights back or displays hurt feelings even when no criticism was intended or made. Those with a destructive narcissistic pattern view allying other than excessive praise as criticism and react to it. For example, if a worker points out an error to the supervisor with the intent of making sure that it is corrected before the product is shipped and the boss berates the worker for being picky and wrong for thinking that the boss would not have caught it, then the boss is overreacting to perceived criticism. Some parents provide a good example of this characteristic, as they feel any suggestion that their child is less than perfect is critical of them as parents.

Lies, distorts, and misleads. These are deliberate acts to keep receivers uninformed, or to push them in the wrong direction, or to insure that they make mistakes. The colleague who withholds needed data or information, the spouse who denies doing something that was done, and the so-called friend who twists your works are illustrations.

Self as the center. The person who immediately wonders about his or her survival when a loved one becomes very ill or dies (the operative word is immediately), every conversation manages to focus on him or her no matter how it begins or what the topic is, always seems to have a life crisis or tragedy, and/or takes some credit for everything others do are some examples for self as the center.

Overcontrolling and blaming. The person who has to know everything that is going on and everything about someone else, including their thoughts, who expect that nothing will be done without his or her permission, and who expects others to do as they are told is someone with characteristics described as "overcontrolling." The words everything and nothing were chosen to convey the absoluteness of the need for control. The person who is overcontrolling discourages any initiative or independence from others. One example of the tendency to be overcontrolling is the top administrator who micromanages. Those who work with him or her are usually frustrated at the lengths to which the person goes to know and direct everything. It is as if others are children who cannot be trusted to wipe their noses when needed. Other workers are not treated as colleagues.

There is a distinct difference between directing and organizing to make sure that tasks are accomplished, and/or that things run smoothly and having to have so much control as to know and direct everything. The first is characteristic of a good manager whether in business or a homemaker. The second characterizes a person who winds up being considered negatively by many who have to interact with the person on a regular basis.

Blaming describes the person who refuses to accept responsibility and almost always blames you, or someone, if some glitch, error, or lapse in judgment occurs. Blame is freely bestowed even when the incident can be shown not to be someone else's fault. For example, if committee members did not receive a notice for a meeting chaired by the destructive narcissist, whose responsibility it was to send the notice, someone else would be blamed even though the mailroom was not asked to send the notices out. The destructive narcissist will directly say or infer that you, or someone else, should have hand-delivered the notices. All efforts to help the person understand what happened are met with statements that you must take steps to see that it does not happen again. What is very frustrating to others is how blame is shifted on to someone else all, or almost all, of the time. Even when an apology is given by the destructive narcissist, it is accompanied with blame on you for putting the destructive narcissist in a position where an apology is necessary or expected. The bottom line is that this person is never wrong.

Hypercritical. Nothing anyone does is ever done right or is satisfactory for this person. There always seems to be something that can be improved, and the need for improvement is constantly pointed out. Having some critical faculties does help to develop improvements, but being overly critical leads to anger and frustration for others. The destructive narcissist may believe that they are only pointing out flaws so that they can be corrected but does not realize or accept that while some criticism may be helpful, they have gone beyond that and are focusing on every flaw all of the time. Further, nothing is ever done to their satisfaction, and others become very frustrated at having themselves or their products always criticized.

Mistrustful, resentful, and envious. The individual constantly questions your and others' motives. He or she seems to always suggest that there is a hidden agenda and that you are not being entirely genuine or truthful. You may find yourself defending your position or opinion quite often and, upon reflection, be frustrated or angry at the need to do so or feel resentful at their putting you in a position where you felt you had to explain, justify, or defend. The individual may also constantly throw out snippets of information calculated to get your reaction, and the information is usually somewhat derogatory to others. For example, the person who usually asks "Why did so and so do or say that?" in response to being told about an event is exhibiting some mistrust. The key word is "usually." Most of us at some time will ask that question, but it is not our usual or general response.

Resentment is expressed by the destructive narcissist quite often, and when examined is usually envy. Destructive narcissists seem to be resentful of the accomplishments and success of others and seek to disparage it in some way. They often make statements that directly or indirectly suggest that the other person achieved because of something other than merit, such as favoritism, special consideration, family or other connections, affirmative action. They usually seize any opportunity to disparage others in some way and usually do it in such a way as to invite others to contribute to it. No one else is deserving of recognition, achievement, and success. Even when they appear to be giving praise, it is accompanied by some piece that is disparaging.

Other behaviors and attitudes that can be descriptive of some people with a DNP include attacking, nagging, opinionated, and closed to the ideas of others.

Attacking. The destructive narcissist understands that the best defense is a good offense and works hard to get his or her licks in first. Thus, many times others will be met with a barrage of questions, charges, and criticisms before he or she can get a word out. The other person is put on the defensive from the beginning. Any attempt to rebut or answer charges is met with a shift in attack. The destructive narcissist also has no compunction against making personal attacks that term what others would consider positive attributes as personal failings that you had better do something to correct.

Attacks can be direct just as described, or, indirect and subtle. The indirect attacks may be recognized as such only in retrospect. That is, it is not until you reflect on the interaction that you are able to recognize it as an attack. During the interaction, you may have experienced uncomfortable feelings that signaled an attack, but you were not conscious of being attacked when it was happening.

Nagging. Constantly prodding for others to hurry up and do whatever someone wants done is usually not conducive to good relationships, whether it is a father prodding a child, a wife prodding a husband, or a boss prodding a colleague or worker. The key word is "constantly." Some follow-up or reminder can be helpful, but anything beyond that is usually nerve-racking.

Having to meet someone else's agenda all of the time leads to withdrawal from that person so that you do not have to hear the same thing over and over again. You are not allowed enough space to do what needs to be done in your time frame and you not only have to meet someone else's time frame but also have to listen to the person ask or tell you about it incessantly.

Opinionated. Having opinions differs in degree from being opinionated. The first allows for differing points of view, the second does not. One who has opinions can also keep their mind open for new information and this allows for the possibility of change. One who is opinionated is just the opposite. No new information will be considered, and there is no possibility for change of perspective.

While mostly everyone does not want to be considered wishy-washy or unable to form an opinion, most of us do want to be flexible and outgoing. The opinionated person is difficult to work or interact with because there is no possibility that anyone else's perspective will be considered. Destructive narcissists can be extremely opinionated, refusing to entertain any new perspectives, facts, or opinions of others. The mere suggestion that they may be in error is enough to enrage or provoke attacks on others.

Closed to the ideas of others. This trait or characteristic also has elements of the items labeled repressive and opinionated. Being closed to others' ideas means that anyone's ideas other than one's own ideas are of no value. There is also a bit of envy of the person who developed the idea. Being closed, envious, opinionated produces a mindset that cannot or will not consider ideas from others. Further, any ideas expressed by others will be discounted or disparaged in every way and the individual who expressed them made to appear and/or feel stupid, ignorant, and incompetent.

HEALTHY ADULT NARCISSISM

The troubling nature of the DNP can also be illustrated by comparison with a description of healthy adult narcissism. Chapter 10 presents some steps you can use to further develop healthy adult narcissism as that is the ideal, and everyone will have some developing left to accomplish. However, it may be helpful for you to have a vision and understanding of how healthy adult narcissism is manifested, its strengths, and even where you may be undeveloped. Narcissism is not all or nothing, is not "wrong," but when undeveloped it can be troubling to your relationships and feelings about yourself, and is capable of becoming more adult and healthier. A brief description for each behavior and attitude follows.

Creativity. This is the capacity for trying, developing, and inventing something new, novel, and different. Talent may play a role, but creativity is possible aside from the usual perceptions of talent. Every aspect of your life holds possibilities for expansion of creativity.

Empathy. An ability to be consciously and mindfully open to another person's experiencing without becoming overwhelmed, enmeshed, or losing the sense of yourself as a separate individual. You are not walled off from others' emotions all of the time, nor are you consumed by these. You can feel what the other person is feeling, but you control your access to them.

An appropriate sense of humor. What is humorous differs from person-to-person, but an appropriate sense of humor means that you are able to laugh at yourself, appreciate life's absurdities and see the humor in them, but do not see humor in people's tragedies, discomforts, differences such as gender or race, or their inadequacies.

Awareness of finiteness. The mature adult with healthy adult narcissism participates in the enjoyment of life regardless of circumstances because he or she is very aware of life's finiteness. Although this awareness can be terrifying at times, it is also the sustaining force for making the most out of one's life.

Responsibility. Everyone has many responsibilities throughout their lives, and most people assume some part of these, but some do not. As a part of healthy adult narcissism, this responsibility is neither debilitating as in overresponsible, or ignored as in lack of responsibility. Responsible adults recognize their obligations, and carry them out even when they would rather be doing something else.

Self-reflection. Self-absorption is an excessive focus on one's self, but self-reflection is an appropriate examination of behavior, attitudes, feelings, motivations, and so on. It is not an excessive focus, it is an effort at self-understanding for growth and development, to increase one's capacity to be empathic, to foster healthy adult narcissism, and to reduce self-absorption.

Wisdom. Wisdom comes through conscious awareness, learning experiences, and an integration of understanding of these. A wise person does not have all of the answers, but he or she can perceive possibilities, alternatives, options, and their advantages and disadvantages. They use past experiences to understand the present and the future, but are not constrained by what went on before. They know what questions to ask, and more important, they recognize their limitations.

Appreciation and enjoyment. Wonder, joy, pleasure, and gratitude enrich life; help cope with adversity; and keeps us connected to the universe. These also affect us physically, emotionally, and relationally. Healthy adult narcissism allows people to stay in touch with the negative, but also stay in touch with the positive.

A sense of direction. It's been said that if you don't know where you are going, you may end up somewhere else. As healthy adult narcissism develops for a person, he or she begins to make choices and decisions designed to produce a life with meaning and purpose, enduring and satisfying relationships, purposeful work, and enjoyment.

A sense of values. These are freely chosen and act as guiding principles for your actions. The operative words are, freely chosen. Values are incorporated early in life and done so unconsciously from the family, the community, and the culture. A part of the process for becoming a separate and distinct individual is to examine your unconsciously incorporated values, and decide what to keep, what to discard, what to adapt, and what new values to adopt. You make conscious decisions about what values to live by, that are your expectations for yourself, not others' expectations, and which will be guilt or shame producing for you.

BASIC PREMISES

Some important premises that guide the description and discussion of a DNP are that you

- are powerless to change the person we consider to be a destructive narcissist;
- do not have the means or the authority to demand that they change to meet your expectations or needs;
- have some lingering aspects of underdeveloped narcissism;
- have the capacity to change your behavior and attitudes;
- must always remember that the destructive narcissist remains unaware of the destructiveness of his behaviors, attitudes, and feelings.

POWERLESSNESS TO CHANGE THE DNP

Much time and energy is wasted in trying to change a destructive narcissistic pattern in someone else. A competent therapist may be able to help effect positive change but only with cooperation from the person, who must be motivated in some way to want and to work for change. Further, even competent therapists need time to effect change and you are not in a therapeutic alliance with the destructive narcissists. You are their children, lovers, spouses, colleagues, employees, or friends. Thus, you are mostly power-less to effect any changes. No amount of love, affection, changes in your behav-ior, confrontation, ranting, and raving, and so forth, will motivate the person to change to be more acceptable to you or even to become less self-destructive.

It is very difficult to accept that you are powerless. A belief that you can effect changes in the destructive narcissist is descriptive of your grandiose fantasies, and these are lingering aspects of infantile grandiosity coupled with a self-image of competency. It is also reflective of an attitude that others are similar to you in important ways, and thus can be reached or touched as you are reached and touched. This belief is also reflective of a lack of true understanding of others as distinct and separate from oneself, a sign of inadequate psychological boundary strength. Reaching or touching some with a DNP may be possible but we have to recognize and accept our limitations in this respect.

LACK OF AUTHORITY

Associated with powerlessness is a lack of authority to demand that the other person change to meet your needs or expectations. You probably do not perceive it as a demand that the other person change, but it is. Many people generally think of it as a sincere desire to help the other person to be more realistic, behave in more constructive ways, to help them recognize others as worthwhile, unique individuals, to show that you value the relationship, or to help that person reduce self-destructive behaviors. Our motives are praise-worthy, we are trying to help the other person.

Many times what you fail to recognize is that your vision of needed changes rises from your own needs and expectations. Yes, the changes may do all that is needed to make the person more effective and loveable, but the impetus is your need to have him or her be this way—not his or her need. The person did not request or seek your assistance to change, you decided it was necessary and began to work to make him or her accept your vision.

The inability or unwillingness to recognize your need as the driving force for having someone change, is associated with an unclear sense of some bound-aries, and some lingering aspects of grandiosity, along with an unconscious wish to "fix," or "save" the other person.

LACK OF AWARENESS

Those with a Destructive Narcissistic Pattern produce much frustration in those with whom they interact because of their indifference to the impact of their behavior on others. They appear to be unaware of just what it is that others object to or find offensive, but even when the impact of these behaviors on others is brought to their attention, will easily dismiss any suggestion that they are less than perfect. Indeed, trying to confront the destructive narcissist generally ends up with the confronter feeling worse than before they approached the topic.

Certainly the defense mechanism of denial is in effect, but the destructive narcissist's defenses are so strong that it is unlikely that anyone will be able to break through the denial. This person is firmly unaware of the destructive nature of his behaviors, feelings, and attitudes.

Those of us who must interact on a regular basis with persons having a DNP need to accept and remember that nothing you do or say will cause them to become more aware of what they are doing and saying, nor will they increase their awareness and concern about the impact of their behavior on others .

PERSONAL DESTRUCTIVE NARCISSIST CHARACTERISTICS

Just as destructive narcissists do not recognize their destructive narcissistic characteristics, so may others, including you, have the same blind spots. That is, you may have some destructive narcissistic characteristics, but nothing anyone does or says makes us accept that we are the way they describe us.

A part of coping with people who have a DNP involves your willingness to be open to self-exploration. The best way to prevent the negative impact of the destructive narcissist is to examine your own underdeveloped narcissism as this may be what is helping to trigger your uncomfortable feelings.

You are encouraged to stay in touch with feelings generated while reading the descriptions and discussions about destructive narcissistic characteristics and to reflect on your behaviors and attitudes. This is one way of engaging in self-examination, and if you just entertain the possibility that you have a form of some of these characteristics that may negatively impact interpersonal relations can be enlightening and informative. It can be the beginning of positive change. Your willingness to open yourself this way increases your awareness of personal behaviors, attitudes, and feelings that can be indicative of destructive narcissism.

CAPACITY TO CHANGE AND COPE

This book is written with the firm conviction that everyone has the capacity to change characteristics that are indicative of destructive narcissism if they are willing to engage in self-exploration and to consider that they may have some level and intensity of behaviors, attitudes, and feelings that are somewhat destructive. There is also the conviction that you have the capacity to constructively cope with the destructive narcissism of others.

Your capacity to change is there if you are willing to tap into its potential and allow yourself to experience the intense and uncomfortable emotions that usually accompany this experience. You may also find untapped sources of strength and creativity that lie dormant. Sometimes the change is painful, and there are times when you need the expertise of a competent therapist to guide and support you through this self-examination and change. A sense of meaning, purpose, and fulfillment can be the reward for undertaking this process.

You also have the capacity to cope with destructive narcissism in others if you are willing to accept your limitations, and your lingering aspects of grandiosity, which prevent you from accepting the destructive narcissist as he or she is. An awareness of your own destructive narcissistic characteristics, and your ability to increase your awareness of how your issues get triggered by interactions with a destructive narcissist also help to increase your ability to cope.

OVERVIEW OF BOOK

Chapter 1, "Who Are These Infuriating and Difficult People?" presents some illustrations to guide readers in recognizing destructive narcissism, and to understand what characteristics describe healthy adult narcissism. This sets the stage for understanding the development of narcissism as self-love that can be healthy, or can be excessive, and destructive.

Chapter 2, "The Destructive Narcissistic Pattern," provides an extended description for the pattern, expected or age-appropriate narcissism, and four types or categories; the Needy narcissist that is infantile in his or her dependency, the Critical narcissist who is suspicious of everyone and everything, the Manipulative narcissist who plays games in relationships and is into deception, and the Exhibitionistic narcissist who is reckless, grand, and always performing.

Chapter 3, "Indifference to Others," describes behaviors and attitudes that show how indifference is exhibited, and how a self-focus is evident. Also presented are the destructive narcissist's inability to distinguish between self and others, and how others' inadequate psychological boundary strength allows them to be exploited.

Chapter 4, "The Inflated Self," gives some examples for grandiosity, arrogance, attention-seeking, and admiration-seeking behaviors. Grandiosity can be portrayed in many ways, but can also have an impoverished side that keeps others from seeing the grandiosity, and this too is presented.

Chapter 5, "Troubling States: Emotions, Emptiness, and Entitlement," tries to describe the restricted, narrow, poverty-stricken, and self-deserving inner states that people with a DNP can have. Others cannot see this inner world, the destructive narcissist remains unaware of his or her inner experiencing, and these internal states can only be inferred from their behavior.

Chapter 6, "How You Contribute to Your Own Distress," discusses some family-of-origin experiences, other past experiences, your personal undeveloped narcissism, and personality that can make you more susceptible, and increase the distress you feel when interacting and relating to a destructive narcissist. Suggestions are provided to guide you in self-exploration.

Chapter 7, "Intense Feelings," illustrates emotional contagion, describes emotional susceptibility, and discusses how you may unconsciously have some negative and intense feelings triggered in interactions with a destructive narcissist. The specific feelings of anger, fear, guilt, and shame are presented including how the milder aspects for these can be experienced.

Chapter 8, "The DNP in Relationships," describes how the person with a DNP can impact others in three relationships; when the parent(s) have a DNP, the colleague and boss with a DNP in the workplace, and the lover or spouse with a DNP. The difficulties in recognizing the pattern, the negative effects on you and others, and the futility of trying to get them to change are discussed.

Chapter 9, "Moderating the Impact of the DNP on You," provides some specific short-term coping strategies. Long-term strategies require that you do some personal development that strengthens your psychological boundaries, resolve family-of-origin issues, complete unfinished business from past experiences, and grow and develop your undeveloped narcissism, and this work takes more guidance than can be provided in this book.

CHAPTER 2

The Destructive Narcissistic Pattern

A very unpleasant and disturbing personal experience led ultimately to the creation of a way to describe people who have numerous and considerable self-absorbed behaviors and attitudes, but these may be lesser in extent and intensity than would be for diagnosing pathology. Nor are those who interact with them qualified or in a position to make a diagnosis. However, the negative impact on others of these self-absorbed behaviors and attitudes is significant and destructive to their relationships, and to others' self-esteem.

The personal experience happened at work where a person in a position of direct authority did and said things that produced considerable distress on almost a daily basis. (For the sake of clarity and anonymity, this person will be identified as Poko, which is neither male nor female. For ease of presentation, "he" will be used.) Conversations with Poko usually resulted in my feeling angry, frustrated, and impotent. Poko lied, gave misleading and inaccurate information, tried to pit unit members against each other by exaggerating and/or spinning any comments they made that could be made to appear negative, attempted to micromanage everything, was critical and blaming, never assumed responsibility for mistakes but off-loaded the blame for them on others, and other demeaning and devaluing actions. Efforts to establish a working relationship were futile and resulted in even more distress for me, and even physical symptoms, such as headaches, began to be experienced.

Because of the atmosphere of suspicion that was established by some actions of Poko, each member of the unit became more isolated, and I had no one to talk with to try and get a realistic appraisal of my reactions. Two incidents started me on the track to understanding Poko's behavior and attitudes, and the realization that what I was experiencing was not unique to me, or entirely due to my lack of development in some areas.

The first incident was at a subunit meeting where I made a casual comment about having to go home and take Tylenol for a severe headache after a conversation with Poko. Whereupon each and every member of the subunit remarked that they too had to do the same, and some noted that it happened on a daily basis. This was the first time that I knew (I suspected but did not know) that others were experiencing some of the same negative effects.

The second incident happened when Poko called me into the office to tell me that he heard that I was angry about a situation in my subunit. He went on to say that I had been angry once last year, and that my being angry now was a sign of emotional disturbance. (My friends and family would say that I seldom get angry, and when I do, I am silent and withdrawn. I do get annoyed or irritated and am not shy in letting others know when this happens. So Poko's charge was not correct.) At that moment something cleared up for me and I genuinely felt amused. Poko was attempting to get me upset to validate the charge. I laughed, and told Poko that he was not qualified to make that diagnosis and I left the office. I told my colleagues what Poko said and they, too, laughed. But, the most validating response was when I told my husband. He just looked at me and said that I was a lot of things, but emotionally disturbed was not one of them.

It was after the second incident that I started to search the mental health/behavioral science literature to get some information about my experiencing with Poko. What became meaningful was the description of the therapist's experiencing and reactions when treating someone with a diagnosed narcissistic personality disorder or someone who, because of his or her behavior and attitudes, was delayed being diagnosed. The therapist's experiences and reactions mirrored the ones I experienced with Poko. This led me to further explore the object-relations and self-psychology literature. I began to better understand what I was experiencing and developed strategies to prevent me from becoming upset and distressed.

The possibility of a subclinical category began to emerge as I learned more about healthy adult narcissism, age-appropriate narcissism, stable narcissism, and pathological narcissism. It seemed feasible that someone could be not quite in the pathological category, but still have some of the troubling behaviors and attitudes. With this in mind, descriptions were developed for what these self-absorbed behaviors and attitudes could be, and these descriptions formed what I began to call a Destructive Narcissistic Pattern (DNP). It also became clearer that people with a DNP were blind to their behaviors and attitudes that were troubling to others and were destructive to relationships. No amount of telling, selling, demanding, or any other actions gets through to them. They are simply cut off from being able to see these aspects of their self.

Once I understood my reactions and was able to identify what was troubling about Poko's behavior and attitudes, everything became much easier to tolerate. I could employ strategies that helped me maintain equilibrium, keep my sense of humor, stop trying to get Poko to become aware of the negative impact of the behaviors and attitudes, and build myself to increase my healthy adult narcissism. My experiences with Poko, my research, consultation with experts, and the success of the strategies all led me to writing books and articles, including this book.

THE DNP ILLUSTRATED

Three cartoons illustrate the destructive aspects of narcissism in adults. One appeared in my local newspaper and shows a man standing in front of a tombstone looking exasperated and saying to the grave, "I guess this means you will not have the report done by Friday." The second cartoon, shows a woman coming into a room where a man is standing on a chair with a noose over his head tied to a light fixture. She says, "Oh, Henry, not my macrame!" The third cartoon shows a man talking to a woman at a party. He says, "Enough about me. Let's talk about you. Have you seen my exhibit at the gallery?"

In the first cartoon the person wants his needs met or agenda fulfilled regardless of circumstances. There is an absence of concern for the other person and shallow emotions are shown. The person who died is unable to please and is being blamed and chastised. The second cartoon also displays a lack of empathy and concern for the other person and also selfishness. This is her possession and should not be touched or used by others. Ignored are the seriousness of the act of hanging, and the despair of the man. She seems to be saying that it's OK to hang yourself if you use something else. The third cartoon illustrates the characteristics of constantly needing to be the center of attention and admiration-seeking behavior.

DESCRIPTIONS AND DEFINITIONS

Destructive and pathological narcissism can be more easily described or illustrated than defined. There is not an agreed-upon definition, but symptoms, such as extreme sensitivity to perceived criticism, slights, a sense of entitlement, the continued failure to develop and maintain satisfying relationships, and so on are behaviors and attitudes that are agreed on as descriptive, and can be used as clues. Other clues are the persistent feelings others have of frustration, anger, incompetence, and many other negative feelings aroused through interactions with them on a regular basis, the significant indifference to others, and a lack of empathy.

Another reason it is difficult to define destructive and pathological narcissism is that it is often confused with or intertwined with self-esteem, that is, how one feels about oneself. Self-esteem is considered to be a part of narcissism but is not the same as narcissism. For example, the narcissist will usually have inflated self-esteem, but that is only one characteristic.

Another consideration is that there appears to be a continuum for narcissism, ranging from expected and age-appropriate to pathological, and this continuum is the premise for much of what is presented in this book. The fourth consideration in trying to define or describe narcissism is that there seem to be developmental stages for narcissism leading to age-appropriate narcissism. That is, what would be considered an appropriate attitude or behavior for a child or infant is not appropriate for an adolescent or adult. For example, it is expected that a toddler will behave in a way that demands the center of attention almost all of the time. The child charms, misbehaves, or cries, to get attention. It is not expected that adolescents and adults will need to be the center of attention almost all the time, and so their unceasing demands for attention are not considered appropriate. Some suggested age-appropriate attitudes and behaviors are discussed later.

What Is a Destructive Narcissistic Pattern (DNP)?

The Destructive Narcissistic Pattern is a concept presented in this book that is intended to describe a group of behaviors and attitudes that are self-absorbed to the point where relationships with others are negatively affected. It is no one particular behavior or attitude, and readers are asked to not think of it as such. The collection of behaviors and attitudes displayed may differ from person to person and, because of the lack of objectivity, it can be difficult to even describe what these people with a DNP are doing and saying that are producing the frustration, anger, and other negative responses in others who have to interact with them on a regular basis. For ease of discussion ten characteristics that are descriptive of a DNP are categorized as follows:

Indifference to others
- Extensions of self and boundaries
- Exploitation

- Lack of empathy

The inflated self

- Grandiosity
- The impoverished self
- Attention-seeking
- Admiration-seeking

Troubling states

- Shallow emotions
- Emptiness
- Entitlement

OVERVIEW OF CHARACTERISTICS

The destructive narcissist can be described as having many or all of the following traits or characteristics, and these are grouped as (1) indifference to others; (2) the inflated self; and (3) troubling states. Each individual with a DNP will differ in the level and intensity of each characteristic, but will usually have aspects that are troubling to others and make it difficult to maintain satisfying relationships. All descriptions are for adults, as children and adolescents are expected to demonstrate these characteristics as a normal part of the developmental process. The following descriptions are brief, and each characteristic is discussed in more detail in subsequent chapters.

INDIFFERENCE TO OTHERS

Extensions of Self

One of the developmental tasks the infant must successfully complete is to become aware of what is self and what is not self. Adults with healthy narcissism are able to distinguish between the boundaries of self and understand what is not self. This sounds very simplistic, but the narcissist is able to relate to the world only in terms of self and is not able to distinguish between self and not self. This is one of the reasons narcissistic rage occurs. The person, thing, or event did not respond as it should as an extension of self. Destructive narcissists assume, as infants, that nothing exists apart from the self.

Everything and everyone is perceived as an extension of self for the destructive narcissist. By being an extension of self, everything and everyone is under the control of the destructive narcissist, exists only to serve their needs, and does not exist apart from the destructive narcissist. Narcissistic rage is experienced in response to an event that shows that someone or something is not under his or her control, and is experienced by everyone at some point, but seems to be chronic with the destructive narcissist.

Exploitation

Giving and receiving are adult expectations. Adults seek ways to get their needs met and ways to meet the needs of others. They are able to adjust and adapt to changing expectations and needs, to delay gratification, to give others priority—such as children's needs priority over their own needs, and to delight in giving as well as receiving. The degree to which destructive narcissists expect others to meet their needs is absolute, and they maintain the position that others have no right to expect them, the destructive narcissists, to meet their needs.

Lack of Empathy

The ability to empathize is one characteristic of healthy narcissism in an adult. Empathy is more than just sympathy for another person. Empathy occurs when one is able to sense accurately the inner experiences of the other person and feel the same feeling, and to not lose a sense of oneself as separate from the other person. Rather than just guessing, hypothesizing or projecting how someone must be feeling, empathy entails being there and having the same feelings. Those with a DNP are not able to empathize as they are only aware of very primitive feelings, such as anger. It is extremely difficult to understand and accept that these persons do not empathize. However, the destructive narcissist does expect empathy from others.

Everyone is expected to show concern and empathize with the destructive narcissist; however, he or she will not show concern or empathy for others. Lack of empathy is one of the significant traits of the narcissistic personality and will be discussed in more detail later in the book. For example, the destructive narcissist feels entitled to show scorn and contempt for others without their retaliating in any way. Those with a DNP have no idea what it feels like for the other person to be the target of scorn and contempt; they only accept what they experience. Under the same conditions, they would tend to discount or dismiss expressions of scorn and contempt.

THE INFLATED SELF

Grandiosity

It is difficult to understand how anyone can consider him or herself to be all-powerful and all-knowing when one is faced with a multitude of situations, people, and things that are unknown, little understood, and certainly not under one's control. However, those with a DNP do not accept these limitations for themselves as do most all other adults. There is a big difference between feeling that you can make a difference and feeling that only you can make the difference.

The destructive narcissist's perception of reality is that he or she is all-knowing and all-powerful, which is also the definition for omnipotence—sort of like the "Great I am" in *The Wizard of Oz*. It is this characteristic that allows the DNP to take credit for work done by others. They truly feel that it was only through their knowledge and power that the work was done and everyone should accept that they, and only they, deserve the credit. If not for them, nothing would have been accomplished.

Need to Be the Center of Attention

Almost everyone enjoys the special feeling that comes from being the center of attention for a brief period. Most people become uncomfortable when attention is focused solely on them for an extended period of time. Toleration of being the center of attention varies from person-to-person, but few want the entire spotlight all of the time. Adults who must have this attention all the time go to great lengths to secure it and become upset when it is not given to them.

Many with a DNP will have a strong need or desire to be the center of attention. These are the people who can always top your situation or story. They had it harder, were more successful, did more, suffered more. They may also go to greater lengths to make sure they are noticed and become anxious if they think the spotlight has shifted away from them. They always seem to be saying, "Look at me! Look at me! Look at me! Now!"

Need to Be Admired and Envied

We get a very good feeling when someone tells us they admire us for some perceived characteristic, deed, or behavior. We tend to value it even more when it is freely given and the person is sincere. Further, we do not feel it is an entitlement; nor do we seek to be admired by everyone. In short, we like it and can get enough. The destructive narcissist demands admiration and never, ever gets enough.

In addition to being the center of attention, these people with a DNP yearn to be admired by everyone. It is not enough to receive admiration from a few; it must come from everyone and be given to him or her all the time. Not receiving constant admiration is very wounding, and those who do not give the desired admiration are ignored, devalued, or dismissed. If you do not give this constant admiration, you cease to be of value and he or she will have nothing more to do with you.

Troubling States

Shallow Emotions

Adults generally experience a wide and deep range of emotions, and many have the ability to express these and are not limited to the primitive emotions of anger and fear. Not so the destructive narcissist who experiences a deprived emotional life where the words are expressed, but the feelings they describe are not available to the person.

An example is the person who expresses pleasure about something, but others find it hard to believe that he or she is really pleased. The real state of affairs may be that he or she cannot feel pleased, so the words ring false.

Emptiness

Adults with healthy adult narcissism will have meaning and purpose for their lives, a deep commitment to some other people and causes outside themselves, a rich emotional life, and feel connected to their self and to the universe. The core of these people's selves is full and rich even when they are struggling or facing adversity. There may be times when they question the current meaning and purpose for their lives, or have lost a meaningful relationship, or their emotional life seems full of negative feelings, or they feel adrift from self and the universe. However, they accept that these states and events are a part of life, and understand that all states are temporary, so they are not cut off from their emotions.

However, the destructive narcissist is empty at the core of self, knows of no other way of being, and assumes that others are as empty as he or she is. This emptiness is terrifying, and many of their actions are attempts to deny, or to prevent awareness of being empty at the core of self.

Entitlement

Even though everyone is unique in the universe, according to the existential theory, this does not bestow specialness. It feels good to be accepted as unique, worthwhile individuals, who are valued. Where the destructive narcissists would demand and feel entitled to have others perceive them as special, those with more stable and healthy narcissism are content if a few people feel this way. Further, they do not feel that they are entitled to have others perceive them in this way but that being considered unique and special is something to be earned and cherished.

A destructive narcissist expects others to fulfill his or her needs but also expects that others will have no expectations from them. In other words, everyone is expected to give the destructive narcissist what he or she wants or may need; however, you should not expect the destructive narcissist to give you anything. These needs may he emotional, psychological, or physical. Destructive narcissists have many needs and the extent to which you can and do satisfy them determines whether the relationship continues.

Strongly connected to wanting to be the center of attention, admired, and entitled is the desire to have others consider him or her as unique and special. They may give lip service to the notion that we all are worthwhile and unique, but they really want to be perceived as being more so than anyone else in the world.

The category Destructive Narcissistic Pattern (DNP) is suggested to describe people who have some characteristics associated with pathological narcissism but may not be fully described or diagnosed as such. They display attitudes and behaviors that are destructive to self and others: they produce frustration in almost everyone who has to interact with them; they devalue others; and they lack empathy. The extent and degree to which the DNP is displayed are less than that of pathological narcissism, but the pattern is very troubling to their relationships. They may function and achieve very well, but have unstable personal relationships, for example, three or more marriages because of divorce. These people can be very shallow, and constantly produce feelings in others of frustration, incompetence, and of being blamed and criticized. As with the pathological narcissist, the destructive narcissist is best known by reactions produced in others from interactions with this person. The descriptions for a DNP, the types and so on, are intended to be illustrative of troubling behaviors and attitudes, and is not a diagnosis.

The focus for this presentation of the DNP is on understanding the destructive aspects of narcissistic characteristics for oneself and others, strategies for protecting oneself from being negatively impacted or influenced by the destructive narcissism of others, and describing the individual who has many or all characteristics of a DNP. First some characteristics for each category of narcissism are described: expected and age appropriate, and undeveloped.

EXPECTED OR AGE-APPROPRIATE NARCISSISM

This has as its basis the psychological growth and development of the individual. Infants are expected to be grandiose and perceive the world as an extension of self. Their experience is that they make things happen, for instance, crying when hungry produces food. They do not perceive mother, or the nurturer, to be a separate and distinct being apart from self, but perceive the nurturer as a part of self and under self's control. As the child grows and develops, he or she becomes aware of self and not self, begins to perceive self as separate and distinct from others, and begins to differentiate between others. Children are taught to share, that others have needs and rights, and that they are not omnipotent. Thus, at each stage of psychological growth and development, the expected narcissism differs and incorporates awareness of others. For example, children are expected to have little sense of ownership or boundaries. They know what is theirs but may also consider what belongs to someone else as theirs also. Adults, on the other hand, are expected to have a clear understanding of ownership and boundaries, and it is not expected that an adult will assume ownership of something that belongs to someone else. Healthy narcissism in adults is demonstrated by creativity, appropriate humor, wisdom, responsibility, self-reflectiveness, and empathy.

An adult with age-appropriate narcissism will exhibit most of the following behaviors and attitudes in addition to many or most of the characteristics of healthy adult narcissism.

Caring, concern, and connected to others
- Self and boundaries
- Respect for others
- Frequently empathic

The aware, accepted and realistic self
- Tamed grandiosity
- Accepts attention
- Appreciates admiration

Positive and helpful inner states
- A rich emotional life

- Recognition that others exist
- An essential core self

CARING, CONCERN, AND CONNECTED TO OTHERS

Self and Boundaries

Others are clearly perceived as separate and worthwhile individuals deserving of respect and not as extensions of self. This perception extends to their children who, while needing nurturing and care, are also allowed to have different opinions, make decisions for themselves, and are guided to achieve separation and individuation from the parent. Others' boundaries are respected, and his or her personal boundaries are strong and resilient.

Respect for Others

Others are perceived as unique and different from oneself, and are to be respected and valued. They are not targets for exploitation and are allowed to make their decisions without undue influences, such as trying to trigger their guilt or shame to get the other person to do what they want. They do not ask for favors without expecting to return them, do not tell or order people (even children) to perform personal services they could do for themselves, do not constantly seek to obtain an advantage, and are respectful of others' time, effort, and possessions.

Frequently Empathic

The adult with healthy narcissism is able to be appropriately empathic and does not become enmeshed, overwhelmed, or manipulated by others' intense feelings. They do not try to be empathic with everyone, nor do they try to be empathic all the time. However, much of the time they *are* empathic, and with many people.

THE AWARE, ACCEPTED, AND REALISTIC SELF

Tamed Grandiosity

The inflated and expansive self is tamed so that a more realistic and integrated self appears. This self is aware of personal limitations, able to accept the flawed imperfect self while still working on improvements, and is able to recognize his or her undeveloped narcissism when it appears. The tamed grandiosity allows for admission of mistakes, that much is not known, and that there are realistic limits on what can be accomplished.

Accepts Attention

This person does not try to be the center of attention all the time, and has little or no discomfort when attention is on someone else. The adult with healthy narcissism does not shun the spotlight when it is appropriate, but does not act to gain all or most of the attention almost always.

Appreciates Admiration

The adult with healthy narcissism enjoys and appreciates compliments, especially when they are genuinely expressed, accepts these, but does not become puffed up or feel superior because of the expressed admiration; is not taken in by flattery and can recognize it as exaggeration and as being insincere; is proud of his or her accomplishments, but not excessively so; and does not seek to bask in the reflected glory of people with status and power.

POSITIVE AND HELPFUL INNER STATES

A Rich Emotional Life

A wide range and depth of emotional experiencing and expression is a characteristic of healthy adult narcissism. These people are not limited to intense negative emotions, but can experience levels from mild to intense such as appreciation, pleasure, happiness, and joy.

Recognition That Others Exist

Respect for personal and others' boundaries, able to meet personal needs, a deep understanding that others do not exist simply to meet their personal expectations and needs, does not demand preferential treatment, and respects and tolerates differences. The ability to delay gratification is an adult characteristic and expectation, as is a willingness to abide by rules, laws, and regulations or changing those that are inadequate or unfair, and an understanding of when others' needs must receive priority.

An Essential Core Self

Adults with healthy narcissism are not empty at their core, but have a self that has meaning and purpose. Although there can be adversity and unhappiness in their life, these adults remain centered and grounded in their beliefs and purpose. They are able to be creative see wonder and beauty and to connect to others and the universe in enduring, meaningful, and satisfying ways.

UNDEVELOPED NARCISSISM

This is a concept used to describe less than total expected or appropriate adult narcissism, and there are several areas where he or she has not fully developed. The individual functions well, has many satisfying relationships, but could also be described as having some more developing to do to have more fully the adult healthy narcissism. Examples for clusters of undeveloped narcissism for a person could be similar to the following:

- Smug, selfish on occasions, and very concerned about his image.
- Says outrageous things to get attention; cocky, and conceited at times, fails to recognize or accept his or her limitations.
- Tells "little white lies" to keep from expressing his or her real feelings or to avoid disagreements.
- Often sarcastic, teases, and jokes; expects others to change their schedule to suit his or her own.
- Takes unearned credit.
- Boasts about his or her spouse's, and children's accomplishments, feels some slight sense of superiority; dresses mainly in designer clothes to get attention and arouse envy; can overcommit his or her time and energy.
- Engages in self-promotion at every opportunity, frequently proposes himself or herself for an award or recognition, will give out misinformation at times to get an advantage.
- Often wonders why everything seems stacked against him or her; quick to point out flaws, mistakes, and imperfections; thinks that others should have high standards like his or hers.
- Is careless about obeying what he or she thinks are silly rules, such as returning library books on time; will volunteer his or her children's time to do chores for others on occasion; can be dreamy or abstract instead of listening to his or her children or spouse and trying to understand their needs.

TYPES OF DESTRUCTIVE NARCISSISTS

Destructive narcissists can be classified into four types: needy, critical, deceptive, and exhibitionistic. The classifications are not mutually exclusive, that is, some individuals may demonstrate one or more characteristics from more than one classification. However, most will have consistent behavior over time that encompasses most or all of the characteristics in one classification, and there can be subclassifications. The need to classify is helpful because it then becomes easier to propose strategies to help you cope. Further, if you identify yourself as tending to become like the described classification, you can then begin to explore both the etiology and needed behavioral changes.

NEEDY NARCISSISTS

Needy narcissists are described by others as dependent, passive-aggressive, draining, and so on. They seek to be "fed" by others and are never satisfied. The more they get, the more they seem to need or want. They cling to others and are very dependent on the approval of others to the point where they become very anxious when they do not get the attention or approval they feel they need.

You can be attracted to the needy narcissist because this person can be very charming at first. You are told in many ways how very important you are to their well-being, and that they are appreciative. It is very seductive to be thought to be necessary to another person's happiness, and you may extend yourself to try to fulfill their every need, and are successful for a period of time.

However, there comes a time when you begin to feel exploited or incompetent because there is no end to their needs. It is impossible to meet all the needs of the other person, especially because the needy narcissist expects you to read his or her mind, know what his or her needs are, and give them without any hesitation. The person may even tell you, "You ought to know what I want without my having to tell you." It is not possible to avoid disappointing him or her under these circumstances, as you cannot always guess correctly. Such a person is very hurt that you cannot meet his or her needs and lets you know this in many ways, leading to your feelings of shame and guilt that you are remiss. Relationships with the needy narcissistic person can be very draining, leaving you with the feeling that you are inadequate because you do not meet the person's needs and that if you were more competent or loving, you would be able to do so.

The interesting thing is that these people do not take action to get their needs met. They tend to sit back and make implicit demands on others with the expectation that others will meet their needs. For example, instead of giving a spouse a list of desired birthday gifts, the person expects the spouse to intuit what he or she would like and to give the perfect gift. Since the spouse is unlikely to be able to accurately guess what is wanted, the gift selected is almost guaranteed to be unsatisfactory.

There is another category of the needy narcissist that adds overt anger to other characteristics and produces behaviors and attitudes similar to that of an antisocial personality. Instead of being passive-aggressive, those in this category are less passive and their anger is easier to observe, although they may not directly express it. These individuals feel that they have been neglected or deprived and that others have a responsibility to make it up to them. They too can never be satisfied and expect others to make it up to them, and also tend to be easily angered or irritated when their unspoken needs are not met. This is in contrast to the other needy narcissist, who is so disappointed that guilt and shame are triggered in others. The individuals in this category, such as those who are easily angered, tend to trigger anger in others more than guilt and shame, as the attitude "You owe me!" does not usually find a sympathetic ear.

CRITICAL NARCISSISTS

There are numerous careers that demand skepticism, suspiciousness, and criticism. Auditors, IRS agents, policemen at every level, judges, and journalists are examples of such careers. Through training and experience, they learn that others are not likely to be forthcoming or to tell the truth. They may have to dig for correct answers or information, to question what they have been told, and to realize that most people will take every opportunity to be perceived in a positive way.

That is the positive side of being critical, skeptical, suspicious, and so on. However, when combined with narcissism, especially destructive narcissism, these traits result in less positive characteristics of jealousy, envy, excessive self-importance, and the tendency to blame others or to ascribe evil motives to them. The major difference for destructive narcissists is that these traits are part of their personalities, not just traits acquired as a result of learning and experience.

Their interpersonal exploitation takes the form of expecting others to be perfect, to refrain from anything that triggers their jealousy or envy, and to be accepting without question any devaluing statements they may make. As with needy narcissism, others are constantly striving to meet the critical narcissist's needs but can never do so completely. Over the long haul, the critical narcissist tends to repel and alienate others because of the constant criticism, blame, and suspiciousness. They can never trust others except on a very limited basis, and this attitude can be detrimental to any relationship.

Critical narcissists remain unaware of the impact on you of their criticizing, blaming, or suspicious remarks, even when these are directed at someone else. You may try to tell them how these constant negative comments about you and others are affecting you and the relationship, but they do not hear this, nor do they change. They may stop for the moment, but are apt to ring up the comments and your reactions again and use these as illustrations of how you don't accept personal responsibility, refuse to admit your mistakes, are not trying hard enough, don't have standards, and so on. The critizing, blaming, nagging, and so on, do not stop.

However, critical narcissists can be overly sensitive to any hint of perceived criticism by anyone, and become extremely upset. This is an example of narcissistic wounding that leads to narcissistic range. These are discussed in more detail in Chapter 7. These people seem to have their antenna tuned to pick up remarks they do not like, remarks they think are critical of them, or are negative in some way. They can be very adept at putting a negative spin on even the mildest comment or action.

The suspicion that others are out to take advantage of them, "get them," or are working against them leads them to question everything and everybody, including those in a close intimate relationship. They want all the details of your interactions, thoughts, feelings, and ideas, and can wonder what you are hiding when you don't voluntarily supply these, or don't provide enough details for them, or forget to mention something. You can have difficulty getting them to accept that you are a separate person.

How were you attracted to someone so critical and suspicious? You probably did not recognize how critical and suspicious they were, and were appreciative of their caution, high standards, decisiveness, and enjoyed their wanting to know so much about you. You mistook this interest for caring, especially if you were hungry or desirous of this attention. Since some of the suspicions he or she voiced were confirmed, you did not recognize that this suspicion also extended to you.

DECEPTIVE NARCISSISTS

Deceptive narcissists incorporate contempt for others, deceit, perception of others as having value only to the degree they can be manipulated or exploited, and a need to "put something over on others" with a resulting glee or exhilaration at having done so. People who have these traits can be very entertaining, charming, flattering, and influential. They are outgoing and gregarious. However, underlying most or all interactions and relationships are contempt, deceit, and manipulation. Such people are always looking for ways to put something over on others and will use almost any means to accomplish that goal.

They lie easily and constantly, even about things that do not matter. When confronted with their deceptions or lies, they shrug it off or turn it back on the other person, saying he or she misunderstood or that it never happened, which is another lie. The constant deception is wearing and frustrating because, of course, there is usually some truth somewhere, and it becomes difficult to separate fact from fiction. They lie or deceive constantly but not always. Others may give up on the relationship with the deceptive narcissistic person because they cannot rely on their ever telling the truth and get tired of trying to separate truth from lies.

An example of lying that served a purpose but was unnecessary, happened to a colleague. He was a new faculty member at a college and had extensive experience in the public sector before becoming a college professor. He requested a Macintosh computer since that was the type he was accustomed to using. The chair of his department told him the college did not support Macintosh computers, only IBM-compatible ones. Any faculty member who had been employed at the college for one or more years would have known that there were Macintosh computers in several faculty offices and there was a Macintosh computer lab in the building—making the statement of nonsupport untrue. However, being new, the faculty member accepted the statement as true. Later that day he happened to be chatting with an associate dean and mentioned that he was disappointed that the college did not support Macintosh computers and that he was going to have to learn a whole new operating system, which would put him behind on his book manuscript, for which he had a contract. Imagine his surprise and dismay when the associate dean told him the college did support Macintosh computers. He then relayed his conversation with the chair, and the associate dean said he would speak with the chair.

Later that week the chair came to the faculty member and told him that there was good news. He, the chair, had talked to the associate dean and convinced him to get the faculty member a Macintosh computer. This was special, just for this faculty member. Needless to say, the faculty member recognized the deception and manipulation tactics. If he had not had the conversation with the associate dean, he would have thought that the chair did something special for him.

Deceptive narcissists derive a great deal of satisfaction from manipulating others to their will. It is not just a game with them, it is their very existence. Others are valued only to the extent to which they can be manipulated and/or exploited. Once others cease their susceptibility to manipulation, they are of no value. This is seen very clearly in social climbers or others who form alliances in order to use people for their own purposes, such as for promotion. Once the coveted state has been achieved, the previously important people are dropped and new alliances are formed.

The satisfaction derived from manipulating others is expanded when coupled with putting something over on others. This is very different from winning. Almost everyone likes winning. Putting something over on others is more akin to tricking others, devaluing them, and showing contempt. What you must remember is that destructive narcissists have manipulation and putting something over on others as constant goals. They are never satisfied and consider everyone fair game.

You were probably attracted to the manipulative narcissist because you wanted to believe their charming lies, especially those that portrayed you as you wanted to be seen. These people seem to be able to tune in to others' needs, and desires, fantasies, and longings, and are then able to use these to manipulate and exploit them. You may even have told them about your longings, and so on because you were convinced that they were interested, and had your best interests at heart. You were trying to be appropriately open, but they took advantage of your openness.

EXHIBITIONISTIC NARCISSISTS

Exhibitionistic narcissists are characterized by a constant need to show-off, reckless behavior, and arrogance. Practically everything exhibitionistic narcissists do is designed to bolster their self-esteem by demonstrating that they are better, can do more, and are above everyone else. These people are those who define themselves by their material possessions, such as clothing and jewelry, and by a disregard for rules and cultural conventions; they convey the attitude that they do not have to account for their behavior should anyone be so crass as to confront them.

They exploit others when they expect or demand that others supply them with whatever is needed in order to show-off. Spending extensive sums on unneeded material possessions that do not give pleasure or satisfaction but are only for others to admire and envy is one example. Demands that the companion or spouse be and stay physically attractive, or discarding the spouse and replacing him or her with a younger, more attractive person is another example. Acting as if rules, laws, and cultural conventions apply to others but not to them is another example, particularly when this is consistent behavior. Taking unnecessary physical risks such as excessive speeding in cars or boats can exemplify reckless behavior. Taking calculated risks should not be confused with reckless behavior. Reckless behavior is part of the person's pattern of behavior, not an isolated event such as taking a risk where the consequences have been considered in advance. The exhibitionistic narcissistic person does not consider consequences, nor does he or she feel that they apply to him or her, and this is a major difference between risk-taking behavior and reckless behavior.

The destructive narcissist who has exhibitionistic traits does not appear to derive pleasure from possessing the items that were obtained to produce attention and envy from others. The key is the reaction of others. For example, assume that you have wanted an expensive sweater, such as a cashmere, for a long time, even years. You finally feel that you can afford to buy one or you receive one as a gift. Most people will feel pleasure and excitement with the sweater, try it on and wear it whether or not anyone else notices. Some get pleasure just from having it because it is what they wanted. A destructive narcissist, on the other hand, would derive their pleasure only from the envious and admiring comments of others. The sweater would otherwise have no value for them.

Exhibitionistic narcissists can be very attractive and exciting. Others are drawn to this person because they to want share the excitement that comes from association or is reflected by being with him or her. This can be especially true when you are not a risk-taker, feel unexciting, and desire to be perceived as the opposite. The charge you get from being the exhibitionistic narcissist can help you lose your usual cautiousness, participate in doing things you do not want to do but are seduced into doing, and may even participate in dangerous undertakings.

CHAPTER 3

Indifference to Others: Extensions of Self and Boundaries, Exploitation, Lack of Empathy, and Envy

EXTENSIONS OF SELF AND BOUNDARIES

One characteristic of destructive narcissists that underlies much of their frustrating behavior and attitudes is the extension of self. It is difficult for others to understand that they act as they do because the destructive narcissist cannot, or does not, adequately distinguish between self and others. This comes across to others as indifference, but it is not so much indifference as it is that they just don't recognize others as separate and distinct from them. It takes a great deal of understanding to recognize that destructive narcissists assume that everything and everyone is an extension of the self, and are either partially or wholly under their control. In addition, there appears to be stages of development in distinguishing self from not-self ranging from the infant whose self is the world and vice versa, to the lingering incompletion of separation and individuation seen in some adults, and this only adds to the complexity when trying to understand the destructive narcissist. He or she can be anywhere along the continuum of the stages of development.

Some behaviors and attitudes that can describe the extent to which others are seen as extensions of self are discussed in this chapter. The discussion focuses on the destructive aspects and outcomes for this characteristic, and is also designed to encourage reflection on how the characteristic is exhibited in you and others who do not have a cluster of troubling behaviors and attitudes as seen in the DNP. These attitudes and behaviors can impact relationships even though one does not have a DNP. Discussed are separation, individuation, and their roles; an inability to distinguish "me" from "not-me;" an excessive need and expectation for control over almost everyone and everything; and psychological boundaries.

SEPARATION AND INDIVIDUATION

Infants perceive the world in terms of self. The self is the infant and the world is the infant. Gradually the infant becomes aware of the extent to which his or her needs are met or frustrated and this, in turn, influences how positive or negative the perception of self and of the world becomes. Over time the child grows and develops to the point where there is an understanding that there are others in the world who are separate, distinct, and are not extensions of self, nor do they just exist to serve the child. This awareness is fostered by the quality of nurturing received and the extent to which the primary caretaker, who is usually the mother, can be emotionally and psychologically available to the child. These two influences have a significant impact on the psychological growth and development of the child.

This process is clearly illustrated by development or lack of development of healthy, or expected, narcissism. Lack of such development can be described partially as a failure to complete the tasks of separation such as, understanding what is self and what is not self, and individuation such as, understanding that you are distinct from me and that I cannot assume you are like me because you are different. Separation and individuation of the psychological self can be delayed or truncated if the child is perceived as an extension of the parents. For example, it is an extension of self if the child is overprotected, or is used to meet the parents' emotional needs. Parents are not usually aware that they are using the child in this way and do so as a result of their own nurturing needs, which were not met by their parents.

Some indices that adults have not adequately completed separation and individuation include the following:

- Becoming easily enmeshed in a parent's emotions.
- Guilt and shame easily triggered.
- Parental wishes and demands take priority over everything else.
- Continuing to act in accord with old parental messages instead of reasoned and free choices.

DISTINGUISHING "ME" FROM "NOT-ME"

One way in which the DNP is displayed is through the perception of where one's self ends. Many destructive narcissists are unable to adequately distinguish "me" from "not-me." They operate on the premise that their "self" or "me" is under their control, and because they are not aware of the "not-me," they constantly seek to exercise control over others, as they do not consider others as separate and distinct individuals. The attempt to control others may result in the person resisting, thus leading to increased attempts to control. Others may fight back or become passive in their resistance, but the relationship is undermined and both parties are frustrated. The person trying to exert control is labeled as a control freak, overcontrolling, anal-retentive, micromanaging, and so on. Some people try to understand the destructive narcissist's need for control and work within those constraints, but become resentful and frustrated because their efforts are not recognized or appreciated, and are usually met with additional attempts to control. Let's explore that situation a little more.

Attempts to meet the control needs of the destructive narcissist are not usually successful, because no one can adequately meet these needs, to fully meet these needs calls for fusion or merger with the person and giving up your self. It works as follows. The destructive narcissist considers you an extension of his or herself, you are not aware of this perception, so you react as if the destructive narcissist knows you are separate and distinct. Then, when the destructive narcissist tries to exert more control, your resentment and frustration are aroused, leading to the destructive narcissist increasing his or her efforts to control you. Here is an illustration of what can happen.

Assume you are working for a destructive narcissist. This person could be a supervisor, manager, department chair, etc. You have been doing your job for a number of years and are very good at it. The destructive narcissist tries to exert more control by assigning you a task you have done successfully many times over the years, telling you how to do it, specifying when you are to do it, and insisting that you do it over and over to the point where you are frustrated, demoralized, and begin to have doubts about your ability. You may even become angry and depressed, and term the behavior "micromanaging." The destructive narcissist is indifferent to the impact of his or her behavior and even if you were to challenge him or her in any way, he or she would manage to turn the discussion around so that you are wrong. The more you protest, the more the DNP seeks to exercise control.

Another example happens quite often with children. They must wear clothes and colors selected by a parent and are not given an opportunity to select for themselves. Everything always matches, and certain colors or styles may not be worn because a parent does not like them. The decision is based on what the parent wants or perceives as attractive apart from what may be a more objective appraisal. The real statement is that their child, an extension of the self, must look a certain way. The parent's control is absolute and the child as an extension of self must conform. This control may extend to every facet of the child's life including his or her name, which could be the same as the parent's name, such as Junior, or a variation of the parent's name, such as Patricia for Patrick.

BOUNDARIES

Boundaries are those internal and unconscious demarcation points or lines that define where "I" begin and "others" end, or vice versa—in other words, lines that define what is "me" and what is "not-me." Personal space is one way of perceiving boundaries. The internal nature of boundaries makes them individually determined, and many people are only aware of their boundaries when they have been violated or invaded by others.

To give you an idea of how important boundaries are to you on an unconscious level, consider how you would feel in the following situations, or similar ones.

- You are working on a report or other task and someone comes in and interrupts you without acknowledging that he or she can see you are busy.
- A boss or supervisor puts his or her arm around you.
- You come home tired, only to find that your spouse has promised a neighbor or friend that you would do a chore for the person.
- When you were a teenager, your parents would come into your room without knocking.
- As a child you were expected to fetch and carry for your parents regardless of what you were doing.
- A spouse or parent routinely goes through your pockets or purse just to see what is there.

These are but a few examples. If you felt angry, annoyed, somewhat taken aback, or upset, then you experienced the lack of respect conveyed by violation of your boundaries. There are other more serious boundary violations such as rape, molestation, and physical and emotional abuse, but these are too complex to adequately address in this book. We focus on the less serious boundary violations that are common for destructive narcissists as examples of their extensions of self.

PHYSICAL AND PSYCHOLOGICAL BOUNDARIES

There are two categories of boundaries: physical and psychological; and four types of boundaries: soft, spongy, rigid, and flexible. Boundary strength ranges from poor to healthy. Physical boundaries are the body and material possessions.

- How far out is your personal space? Do you consider your body or parts of your body to be inviolate areas where others must, or should, ask permission before touching? Do you become uncomfortable when someone, especially someone you do not know or do not like, stands or sits too close to you?
- How do you feel when someone uses a possession without asking permission? How would you feel if your home was burgled? These are but a few examples of physical boundaries.

Psychological boundaries are those that define you as separate and individuated from others, and provide the sense of knowing where you begin and others end, or where you and others are different. Personal, or territorial, space is also a psychological boundary. The person who becomes irate because someone sat in his or her chair is demonstrating a psychological boundary. Making unsolicited personal remarks, criticisms, etc., is, or can be, a violation of a psychological boundary. Getting your feelings hurt is an example of an invasion of your psychological boundary. These psychological boundaries arise and develop over time, and few are consciously aware of the level and extent of their psychological boundaries.

Soft boundaries are those that are merged with others' boundaries. Ask yourself the following questions.

- Do you find it difficult or impossible to say no, and/or to follow through on it?
- Do you think that you have too much empathy?
- Are there times when you find yourself caught up in others' emotions and it's hard to let go of them?
- Do you wish that you were not so easily influenced by others' emotions?

- Do you sometimes think that others take advantage of you because you are softhearted?
- Is it almost impossible, or impossible, to not feel you have to do something to help another person feel better when he or she is in distress?

If you answered all or most of these questions positively, then you are likely to have soft boundaries. You do not have a clear sense of where you end, of the boundary that separates you from others, and because of this you are greatly susceptible to emotional contagion.

Neither you, nor anyone else, have too much empathy. What you have is poor boundary strength. Having empathy means that you can feel what the other person is feeling *without* losing your self as being separate and distinct. This means that you cannot have too much empathy, and that you can empathize but can also let go. Empathy is discussed in more detail later in this chapter.

People with soft boundaries can be aware that they seem easy to manipulate and exploit, wish that they could stop being so easily influenced, resolve to not let it happen again, but they seem helpless to prevent it. They can think that preventing being enmeshed or overwhelmed is a matter of willpower, but it is not. The problem is the failure to adequately develop sufficient psychological boundary strength. There are some short-term coping strategies that can be used while working on your boundaries, but these do not substitute in the long-term for building sufficient boundary strength.

Spongy boundaries are a combination of soft and rigid, much like the surface of a sponge. What gets in and what is blocked are not under the person's control as is the case with flexible boundaries. Spongy boundaries permit more emotional contagion opportunities than do rigid boundaries, but less than do soft ones.

What can be distressing for people with spongy boundary strength is that they don't know what to let in or to keep out, have little or no control over this, and are constantly wondering what they did wrong, failed to do, or could do to prevent becoming enmeshed or overwhelmed by others' emotions, or to be more appropriately receptive and not close off possible opportunities for meaningful connections.

Your boundaries may be spongy if you constantly encounter the following:

- Others tell you that you are wishy-washy and they have difficulty knowing when you can be approached.
- You wonder why you let some people take advantage of you.

- You have difficulty resisting being manipulated even when you know that is the person's intent.
- You frequently think you can connect to someone, but are unable to.
- There are times when you feel walled off from others.
- You are more susceptible to emotional contagion than is comfortable for you.
- You feel uneasy and apprehensive about the possibility of enmeshment or becoming overwhelmed by others' emotions.

Rigid boundaries are those, where the individual is so closed or walled off that no one can connect or get close to them, either physically or psychologically. This is often the case when one has been physically, psychologically, or emotionally abused. These people are fearful of being hurt, do not know who can be trusted, and are unable to feel safe, so they retreat, put up barriers and do not allow anyone to get physically or psychologically close. There are also individuals who have selective rigid boundaries that serve the same purpose, to protect from harm or potential harm. Selective rigid boundaries are those that are in effect depending on time, place, and/or circumstance. For example, you may not feel threatened when X sits next to you at a party and puts his arm behind you along the back of the chair or sofa. However, you may feel threatened if someone you do not know does the same thing in an airport waiting room. Another example of a selective rigid boundary is how you feel about others borrowing personal possessions without first asking permission. You may be accepting of this behavior from a spouse but not from a neighbor or coworker.

If your boundaries are rigid, it's because you have learned through experience that you are emotionally susceptible, subject to manipulation, and exploitation, and find that you do things you do not want to do when you soften your boundaries and let someone get close to you. You've been disappointed often and are unable to judge the genuineness of others, so you keep everyone out.

Flexible boundaries are similar to selective rigid boundaries but are more under the person's control. The person decides what to let in and what to keep out, are resistant to emotional contagion, manipulation, and are difficult to exploit. When your boundaries are flexible, you make choices about what you will or will not do, are able to say no and stick to it, do not have your shame and guilt easily triggered by others who are trying to manipulate you, nor do you frequently find yourself doing things you do not wish to do.

Flexible boundaries allow you to give and receive support, and others are not automatically walled off or held at a distance. They allow you to respect and accept yourself as well as to accept and respect others as distinct and separate from you. The ultimate, of course, is having unconditional positive regard for yourself and others, a state to be worked for but seldom, if ever, achieved.

IDENTIFICATION OF BOUNDARY PROBLEMS

Once you have identified any problem areas, you can make specific changes in your behavior that will convey respect for others' separateness, and individuality, and reduce your unconscious extensions of self. You can do such things as the following:

- Ask permission of others to borrow or pick up their possessions.
- Knock and wait for permission to enter a room, even for children's rooms.
- Cease making comments about others' physical characteristics unless invited by them to do so.
- Do not assume you may touch someone without their permission.
- Make a conscious effort to respect children's boundaries and teach them to establish boundaries for themselves.
- Refrain from telling insensitive jokes; eliminate racial and sexist joking.
- Refrain from rifling through your spouse's or children's belongings.
- Let others speak for themselves.

The other side is that you can use these same items to determine how and when your boundaries are violated. You may already know on a nonconscious level, but now you can be conscious of the violation(s) and your feelings about it. Putting a stop to the violations may be as simple as asking someone to please stop a particular action, for example, agreeing to do something that involves you without asking you, or asking that the person knock before entering your office.

You may also want to examine your boundaries to see whether they are either too flexible or too rigid. Either way, they may be having an unanticipated effect on your relationships. These are also issues that may benefit from your working with a therapist to develop useful and sound boundaries that enhance your self but do not exclude or wall off others.

A final word about boundaries. If you have to interact on a regular basis with a destructive narcissist, you will find it helpful to have very clear boundaries as to where you begin and where the other person ends. You need to establish these boundaries and make them very clear to the destructive narcissist so that you openly declare that you are separate and distinct—not an extension of the destructive narcissist's self. The destructive narcissist is not free to barge in on you, borrow your possessions, or take over your space. The section on lack of empathy provides some short-term nonverbal strategies you can use to prevent emotional contagion and/or reduce your emotional susceptibility in certain situations, or with certain people. It is wise to be judicious in your use of these as they do convey a lack of empathy. However, if being what you think is empathic causes you to frequently be manipulated and exploited, then you are not really being empathic, your boundaries are not sufficiently developed so that you can be appropriately empathic. You may want to try some of these nonverbal behaviors as strategies under appropriate conditions while you work on strengthening your boundaries.

EXPLOITATION

The need to control others because they are an extension of self is also related to the characteristic displayed by the destructive narcissist of exploitation. Interpersonal exploitation occurs when others are used to satisfy personal needs and desires without consideration for their rights or personal integrity. Others are perceived as valuable only in terms of what they can give or do. They are not inherently valued as worthwhile, unique individuals; they are more apt to be perceived as extensions of self and thus are to be used, or exploited, in the service of the self.

One obvious example is children who are ordered to do what a parent says or wants, without question or hesitation, and may be punished for not being prompt or for making an error. Children may be expected to interrupt what they are doing, for example, playing a game, to go and get something from another part of the house because the parent does not feel like moving. Quite often, the personal integrity of children is not respected.

The destructive narcissist often frustrates and demeans others by giving orders and expecting others to "hop to it." Even when working with colleagues or peers, destructive narcissists give orders and do not seem to understand why the behavior is met with resentment and resistance.

Examples of interpersonal exploitation can also be seen in power exploitation and social exploitation. Power exploitation occurs when an individual has achieved a position or status where their needs have priority and others must fulfill these needs regardless of the effort, discomfort, or disruption necessary to do so. The boss or supervisor who calls you at home with a query that could have waited until you came to work, the spouse who tells you to pick up the dry cleaning even though it is miles out of your way but is located near where he or she works, the committee chair who demands that you pick up refreshments for the meeting knowing that you have to take the children to their grand-mother's first and that picking up the refreshments is out of your way and requires three stops, etc., are illustrations of power exploitation. These people feel they have a right to these services by virtue of their status or position.

A personal experience exemplifies this characteristic for me.

A colleague asked if I knew where a particular key was. Since I knew, I told her where it was, in an office down the hall. She then responded, "Run and get it for me." I exercised enough restraint to just respond, "No." Although she was not in a supervisory position, it seems obvious that she considered herself in a power position where others were expected to attend to her needs.

Social exploitation occurs when someone is flattered, receives deference, and is admired for the ability to confer social importance by association. For example, the CEO who is invited to an event because his or her attendance speaks of the importance of the event, not because he or she is wanted as an individual. They are valued only in terms of the prestige associated with them, not as particular persons. If they should ever leave the position, lose their money, or change circumstances in some way, they will be dropped because their presence no longer conveys prestige or social importance. Name-dropping is another example of social interpersonal exploitation.

LACK OF EMPATHY

Empathy and sympathy have some aspects in common but are very different. Empathy refers to an understanding and experiencing of the inner world of the other person. You feel his or her pain, despair, happiness, and so forth. While experiencing empathy, you do not become one with him or her, you maintain your separateness and individuality, but you also can "feel what is felt by the other." This experiencing allows for an understanding of what the other person is going through and, when properly conveyed to him or her, can produce a bond of trust and safety. The other person can accept that you are not out to harm him or her.

Sympathy means you understand enough of what the other person may be experiencing to be kind, tactful, and give expressions of support, but you do not enter his or her inner world nor experience the same feelings. Further, sympathy is usually given for some unpleasant event, while one can empathize with pleasant events as well as unpleasant ones.

Empathy allows us to understand human conditions, such as anxiety and de-spair, and to make connections with others, thereby reducing alienation and isolation. Increasing our capacity to empathize increases our feelings of belonging and connectedness. Lack of empathy from a person, especially failure to respond empathically, can produce feelings of being misunderstood, devalued, shamed, and/or guilty, as if the other person does not find you worthy or as if you are so fatally flawed as to be different from others. This can be very wounding and, while it may be rationalized or explained, it still has an impact.

This is not to say that we must be empathic to everyone all the time. Not only would this be extremely wearing, but it is not possible. People working in positions requiring extensive empathy, such as mental health professionals, physicians, nurses, ministers, teachers, etc., find that they suffer from burnout when they try to be "fully there" and empathize fully with everyone.

However, the destructive narcissist is characterized by lack of empathy or empathic responses. This person is so task focused and/or self focused that there is little or no awareness of what others may be experiencing. The cartoons described in Chapter 2 illustrate the single-mindedness of the destructive narcissist. The true incident described next also illustrates a destructive narcissist's lack of empathy. Some characteristics have been changed to protect identity of the participants.

A nontenured professor was approaching his pretenure review process date when a series of events intervened. He was hospitalized with severe depression and treated for several weeks. During this period relatives assisted with day-to-day living necessities. While still in the hospital, he received a call from the department chair. The chair asked about the prognosis and when he was expected to get out of the hospital and return to work, and reminded him that his credentials for pretenure review were due in the chair's office that Friday. When the professor pointed out that he was in the hospital, said he could not get the credentials completed, compiled, and submitted in the chair's office by Friday and asked for an extension. The chair responded that he knew the professor was in the hospital and hoped he felt better soon, but the papers were due by Friday. This response was neither empathic nor sympathetic. The rules and time line for pretenure review were not so rigid that additional time such as a week or two could not be granted.

ASSESSING YOUR EMPATHIC BEHAVIOR

The following behaviors can be considered as indicating a lack of empathy in an interaction. Each behavior and attitude has both negative and positive aspects. The negative aspects refer to what is conveyed and perceived by the other person when these behaviors are exhibited. The positive aspects of these behaviors, although as a group they convey a lack of empathy, are that they are useful under certain circumstances. In other words, while it is desirable to be empathic or have a capacity for empathy, you are expected to always be empathic with everyone.

1. Failing to maintain eye contact when talking.
2. Turning away from the other person when he or she is speaking.
3. Leaning backward when interacting.
4. Slumping in the seat when interacting.
5. Responding to content in interactions.
6. Changing the topic if you, or the other person becomes intense.
7. Telling the person what he or she "should" or "ought" to do.
8. Giving unsolicited advice.
9. Focusing more on task accomplishment than the relationship.
10. Ignoring emotionally laden remarks or topics.
11. Becoming bored in interactions.
12. Tending, or trying, not to listen to him or her.
13. When someone is telling you about his or her problems, considering this to be a personal failing on the person's part.
14. Providing solutions to problems before fully understanding them.
15. Rushing to "fix" the person so that he or she does not feel so intensely.
16. Pointing out the negative side for almost everything.
17. Asking lots of questions in interactions.

Failing to Make Eye Contact

When eye contact is not maintained while talking to most other people, some discomfort exists with either the person or the topic. In the United States, not looking someone in the eye and maintaining contact is perceived negatively by the other person. You can be perceived as shifty, lying, insecure, or as trying to hide from the other person. Further, failure to maintain eye contact means that you are ignoring or failing to recognize what the other person is experiencing.

Some people may become uncomfortable when eye contact is held too long. Sustained eye contact is associated with intimacy, and you do not want to be intimate with everyone, nor do you want everyone to perceive you as desiring intimacy. Further, too much eye contact is an individual matter, and the extent to which it is comfortable differs from person to person. What may be comfortable for one person may be very uncomfortable for another person. Cultural differences also impact use of sustained eye contact. In some cultures it is a sign of respect for the others' status not to look the person in the eye.

Turning Away from the Other Person when They Are Speaking

The negative perceptions aroused by failure to maintain eye contact are intensified when your body is not aligned with the other person and/or you do not turn to face the person when he or she is speaking or when you are speaking to the person. This physical attending behavior signals a lack of interest in the other person. A positive for this behavior is that it can reduce the impact of your emotional susceptibility.

Leaning Backward when Interacting

Backward lean is associated with retreating from the speaker, becoming aloof and detached, and/or feeling repelled by the speaker of topic. The body position may also be perceived as exhibiting superiority. It is the reverse of a slight forward lean, which conveys interest and attentiveness.

Slumping, Crossing Arms

Defiance, resistance, hostility, and lack of respect are some of the attitudes conveyed by slumping in the seat when talking or listening and by crossing arms. When you slump in your seat, you cannot exhibit physical attending behaviors, while crossed arms show a desire to maintain distance between you and the other person.

Nonverbal Inattentive Behaviors

Turning away from the other person when they are speaking, leaning backward when interacting, and slumping in a chair are overt signs of inattentiveness and disinterest. Even when you are accurately conveying your feelings by engaging in these nonverbal behaviors they are scant justifications for using them. If, on the other hand, you are using them but are unaware that you are doing so and become aware of your nonverbal behavior, you can use this awareness to find out what is causing this lack of interest on your part. For example, are you uncomfortable with concerns, or are you tired or ill? Becoming aware of what you are doing can give you information about yourself and/or the relationship with the speaker. Incidentally, these nonverbal nonattending behaviors can be used effectively when working on building your boundary strength to prevent emotional contagion.

Responding to Content

The most important part of any communication is the meaning, which is contained more in the feeling part of the message than in the conveying part, and responding to it shows the other person that you understand, or want to understand, him or her. When the response is made only to content, the other person is more apt to feel that you did not hear his or her message, do not have any interest, or do not understand him or her.

Responding only to content may be appropriate when there is a need for quick action, such as in a crisis or danger. Understanding what is meant so that needed action can be taken is more important under these circumstances than trying to understand feelings or empathize. Another circumstance when response to content may be preferable to empathetic responses is when directions or guidelines for accomplishing a task are being given.

Changing the Topic

Strong or intense emotions of others may make you anxious, and in the effort to reduce your anxiety you change the topic to one you feel may be less emotional for the person. This is an understandable response, especially if you have no desire to deal with the other person's feelings, are not tuned in to your own anxiety, or do not know what to do or say in face of the other person's emotional display.

However understandable changing the topic may be, the behavior still conveys a lack of interest in the other person and a desire to distance yourself from his or her intense emotions. This is a form of ignoring the other person and demonstrates a lack of empathy. The time and place may be inappropriate for expressing intense emotion. Loss of control may be an issue, and changing the topic allows control to be established. Some people may get obsessed and/or become mired in their emotions. A change of topic can help bring them to a point where they are better able to cope.

Telling People What They Should Do

"Shoulds" and "oughts" are closely tied to producing shame and guilt. Actions, attitudes, and feelings are embraced or denied with resulting feelings produced by old parental messages that contribute to our self-perceptions.

Doing, thinking, or feeling something because "it is the right thing to do or feel" is not being authentic or honest. The action, thought, or feeling does not occur because of some real conviction or deeply felt value, but because it would be more difficult to accept yourself otherwise.

Giving Unsolicited Advice

The receiver of unsolicited advice is expected to be appreciative and to act on the advice, and if the person does not do so, then he or she will be considered an ungrateful wretch and deserving of failure or unpleasant occurrences. While the giver of the unsolicited advice may not consciously have these feelings, all too often this is the attitude that is conveyed to the receiver. Giving unsolicited advice can also indicate that the giver is not fully understanding the receiver; is uncomfortable with the emotions surrounding the receiver that are triggered within him or herself; wants to appear more knowing or more powerful; feels superior to the receiver and/or is discounting the receiver and his or her needs.

However, when someone is about to engage in harmful behavior it can be helpful to advise otherwise, especially if the person is unaware of the potential harm. Sometimes the unsolicited advice is very informative, and it is particularly easy to accept if given along with the expectation that the person is free to ignore it.

Focusing on the Task

When the primary focus in interactions is on the task rather than the relationship, there is the real possibility that unintentional wounding can occur. Just as in any other message, feelings play an important role, and what was done or said is not as important as how the parties feel about it. A focus on task can make the other people feel as though they are immaterial, and most people do not have positive feelings about being put in that position.

There are times when it is important to get the task accomplished. For example, at a meeting it may be more important to stay focused on agenda items and making decisions than to be empathetic. There are other numerous times when the task takes priority over empathy.

Ignoring Emotionally Laden Material

Ignoring emotionally laden material is risky. Not only may the most important part of the message be missed, but an opportunity to strengthen a relationship may also be missed. When you ignore the underlying feelings or the expressed feelings, the speaker can be left with the impression that he or she is not being heard or is being discounted or devalued in some way. It is as if the speaker's feelings are unimportant.

Others may try to trigger certain responses in us, such as anger, and it may be more prudent to ignore rather than to respond. Another instance where ignoring maybe advisable is in the case of inappropriate timing and circumstances where the remark is made or topic introduced. Many family gatherings have been spoiled because certain topics were explored that would have been better ignored.

Becoming Bored in Interactions

Boredom is difficult to conceal. The speaker is usually aware of the listener's inattentiveness, and this can arouse hostility and other reactions. Boredom usually emerges in response to suppression of hostile feelings. You do not want to be doing or hearing what is going on. The response is not necessarily to what is being experienced or who is talking; it can be a response to something entirely unrelated, as in displaced hostility.

However, when experienced as an interaction, it can affect that interaction in negative ways.

Not Listening to the Speaker

The most obvious negative aspect of tending to tune something out is that important information and statements about the relationship are likely to be missed. Another negative is that the speaker can feel that the tuning out is a desire on your part to terminate the relationship and/or that you cannot, or will not, empathize.

Tuning out may be a way of defending yourself against attacks and negative feelings. While it may be more productive to try to work through these feelings, there are individuals, for example, destructive narcissists who arouse such strong negative feelings that you may be better off not listening to them.

Looking for Personal Failings

Looking for or pointing out personal flaws or failures on the other person's part is usually not received as a positive act. Most people do not appreciate being considered or told that they have character flaws or that they have failed in some way. This also plays into lack of empathy by focusing on content and not feelings. The person may indeed be flawed, but will not feel you understand what he or she is experiencing if you consider whatever happened to be the result of a personal failing, and it is very difficult to successfully conceal this opinion.

Providing Solutions to Problems

Trying to give a solution to a problem before fully understanding it can lead to complications and errors. In addition, this rush to solve may cause the other person to feel overwhelmed and inept, and most of all, to feel that you do not care enough to try to fully understand. Solving the problem may be very important, but understanding the feelings around the problem may be even more important.

Rushing to "Fix" the Person

Akin to providing solutions is the effort to "fix" someone in order to make him or her feel better. What is usually happening is that you want the person to stop feeling whatever he or she is feeling so that you do not have to see or feel that distress. You feel uncomfortable with the intense feelings, so you soothe (fix) the person's feelings. The other person is very aware of your discomfort and the fact that you are more in tune to your feelings than you are to what he or she is experiencing.

Pointing Out the Negative Side

A focus on the negative side, especially if it is being ignored or is unseen, can provide a needed dose of reality. However, if this is a usual response, others begin to feel as if you can never see the positive side of anything and to avoid interactions with you. Highlighting negative points can make others feel as if you are unable to empathize with their positive feelings.

This behavior is similar to giving unsolicited advice. There are times when the other person may not be aware of the negative or downside, and the lack of awareness could lead to significant mistakes or even danger. It can be helpful to make someone aware of a negative aspect not previously considered so that he or she can take it into account when making a decision and make a more informed one.

Asking Lots of Questions

Questioning behavior can make others feel attacked. A barrage of questions can be overwhelming and perceived as trying to put them "on the spot." Games, such as one-upmanship, are played through questioning behavior, and the receiver can be made to feel as if he or she is incompetent or inadequate by the type and number of questions asked. Further, questions are usually asked to elicit facts, while the most important parts of the message are the feelings around the message.

Some of the behaviors and attitudes associated with lack of empathy also have a positive side. That is, when used or experienced under certain conditions, lack of empathy can serve or be perceived in positive ways. Please remember that even experienced therapists cannot always be empathetic; and few, if any, can be consistently and constantly empathetic, so it is not realistic to expect to be empathic with everyone, or to be empathic all the time.

SUMMARY

There are two important points to remember about empathy. The first is that empathy is a characteristic of healthy, age-appropriate narcissism in adults. Real empathy means that you are able to focus on others and sense what is being felt without losing your own sense of self. The self's integrity is maintained and they connect with others in a meaningful way.

The second point is that destructive narcissists lack empathy. They have the words but not the feelings. It is not that they choose not to empathize; they cannot empathize. Empathizing is threatening, as they fear their self will be engulfed or destroyed. They are not able to let go enough to connect with others.

Becoming aware of your lack of empathic behavior is also important. How and when you are insensitive to what others are experiencing and what impact this has on your relationships are very important questions for you to consider if you want to become more empathic. One way of becoming more aware is to try and objectively review your behaviors exhibiting lack of empathy. These are also suggested behaviors that you can decrease that will improve your skills in listening for feelings, thus increasing your empathy.

Therefore, it is not recommended that you try to empathize with the destructive narcissist. When you open yourself to try to experience the destructive narcissist's inner world, you also leave yourself open to his or her projections and projective identifications. You may find that when you try to understand the destructive narcissist's perspective, you end up feeling frustrated, angry, incompetent, and other distressing feelings. In addition, you will most likely find that the destructive narcissist does not ever try to empathize with you. It is a situation where you give much of yourself with little payoff or return.

The list of behaviors can also be used to help you develop some emotional insulation against the emotional sending of the destructive narcissist, where your boundaries allow you to become enmeshed or overwhelmed, and you can find it difficult to let go of these. Even if you are in a field where empathizing is expected and/or you want to be as empathic as possible, you do not have to empathize with everyone all the time. Not empathizing is especially beneficial under certain conditions, and protecting yourself from the powerful negative feelings of the destructive narcissist that are unconsciously projected into you fall into that category. The destructive narcissist's therapist can choose to empathize, but no one else has to empathize.

ENVY

Envy carries with it attitudes of superiority and contempt. Envy occurs when someone wants what another person has, feeling more deserving of it than the other person, can feel cheated because he or she does not have it, and denigrates the person who has what is desired. Wanting what someone else has is not necessarily envy, but when it carries the negative feelings about the other person; such as thinking that the person did not deserve or earn it, or that the person is inferior, then it becomes envy.

Envy can be distinguished from jealousy. With jealousy the fear is the loss of a relationship. Envy can be about status, possessions, reputation, family, and almost anything, but is associated with feeling that the person who has what is wanted is undeserving and/or inferior, and the superiority of the person who does not have it but thinks he or she is more deserving.

The interesting paradox is that a person with a DNP envies others as described above, but also wants to be envied, and very often is achieving and successful. However, for the person with a DNP it is not enough to achieve or acquire possessions, others must feel cheated that they don't have what the destructive narcissist has. Both states exist in the same person, and their feelings of superiority are bolstered when they think or know they are envied.

It would be remiss to not note that there are occasions where people do get something they do not earn or deserve, and when people do not get what they do earn and/or deserve. The latter are cheated and treated unfairly. When this happens to you it can be very upsetting and even enraging. It is not helpful to be told that nothing in life is fair, to not fret, or that you are not alone as this happens to others. If you have ever experienced something like this, and I hope that these times have been few and far between, then you have some understanding of what someone with a DNP experiences almost all the time.

This state is chronic for them, and they can always find numerous examples to envy.

What are some indicators of feeling envious?

- Constant denigration of others.
- Continually boasting and bragging about what one has, accomplishments, and so on.
- Feeling cheated when others are successful, and so on.
- Self-aggrandizement.
- Bemoaning the absence of something and wondering why others seem to have more.
- Dissatisfaction with what one has, as others who do have what is desired are not as worthy.

CHAPTER 4

The Inflated Self: Grandiosity, The Impoverished Self, Attention-Seeking, and Admiration Seeking

The inflated self is seen in some behaviors and attitudes of the Destructive Narcissistic Pattern. Discussed in this chapter are grandiosity, the opposite of the inflated self—the impoverished self, attention-seeking, and admiration-seeking.

Grandiosity is difficult to describe as some of the descriptors are not necessarily negative, and others are so vague that they cannot be easily described. The term is used here for people who have inflated and excessive self-esteem to the point where:

- Others are thought to be inferior and inadequate, and are treated and responded to so as to convey these perceptions.
- They do not have a realistic perception of their abilities and limitations, thinking that they are more capable and able than the evidence will support.
- They fantasize and desire envy from others because that envy shows the recognition of their superiority and others' inferiority.
- Almost everything that happens is reacted to with a self-focus.

- They assume that their superiority entitles them to determine what is best for others, what others should do or be, and to have their decisions about others carried out.
- Terms such as, cocky, conceited, and arrogant seem to fit them.

Babies and children have considerable grandiosity and, with careful nurturing, gain a more realistic perception of self that has adequate self-esteem, which is not inflated or excessive, and which recognizes the existence of others in the world as self-determining individuals. Adults who do not adequately complete this process continue to perceive themselves with grandiosity, and are related to others in terms of this infantile grandiosity. Let's look at a few examples.

- The woman who finds some way every time she interacts with her sister to tell her that she isn't doing something right, that she always seems to do things wrong, her appearance isn't up to the standards the woman expects, and that she doesn't understand why her sister cannot do better.
- Supermom; superwoman; superman.
- Men and women who rationalize their failure to receive an award, a promotion, a bonus, or the like because others are envious and don't want to see them succeed.
- A man speaking about his wife says, "Jane has gone and died on me. Now, what am I going to do?"
- Executives, such as film producers and directors, who assume they have the right to sexual favors on demand from employees and/or aspiring employees.

Egocentric and selfish are terms used to describe someone or an action that conveys that he or she is the most important person, and discounting or devaluing others. Sometimes the terms egocentric or selfish are used to manipulate others because few adults want to be described this way, and calling someone egocentric or selfish is intended to make the person feel shamed and so change their behavior. The opposite descriptors, such as the ability to consider others' needs, delay of self-gratification, and empathy, are indicators of maturity.

When one is egocentric or selfish there is usually a discounting or devaluing of others' needs, which results from a lack of empathy. The focus is only on the self, with little or no awareness or attempt to understand needs others may have. Indeed, even when others clearly state their needs, they are not heard or their needs are minimized in some way.

GRANDIOSITY IN CHILDREN THAT LINGERS FOR ADULTS

The destructive narcissist always has him or herself as the focus or center of the universe. Those with a DNP typify the statement, "I am the great I am," as is also seen with infants and children. Everything and everyone are extensions of self, their "self" is all there is. Some with a DNP who have achieved some measure of separation and individuation will be aware of others in the universe, but may consider others as being there to service them. Those with a DNP consider themselves immune from all criticism and feel that they should receive all recognitions and rewards. Grandiosity, as described earlier, is one of the characteristics of the DNP and appears in many forms and on many levels.

Grandiosity is what allows people to feel they have a right to control others, to violate their boundaries, to have all the answers, and to be arrogant and conceited. In object-relations and self-psychology theories the infant and the child are expected to be grandiose as they are largely unaware of anything or anyone as separate and distinct from self. They gradually become aware of self as separate and distinct from not-self and begin to separate and individuate. As this process occurs, grandiosity lessens and awareness develops of others' rights, needs, and boundaries. The destructive narcissist appears to be stuck in this process, but many adults not characterized as having DNP exhibit aspects of grandiosity that continue to linger from childhood. Almost everyone has some lingering aspect of grandiosity, even though it may show itself very infrequently and in subtle ways. It may also be termed different things, such as hubris, overconfidence, or false pride.

Many people without a DNP can exhibit lingering aspects of grandiosity. These behaviors and attitudes point to the degree to which expected grandiosity for an infant and in childhood has grown, developed, and has been integrated into "self." Infants and children who do not adequately integrate grandiosity tend to maintain a more infantile sense of grandiosity, and as they develop into adults, usually have destructive, closet, or even pathological narcissism. There are levels and graduations of grandiosity, and the characteristic is tied to developmental stages. Lingering aspects of grandiosity are those aspects carried over into adulthood and action, usually on a nonconscious level. Almost everyone has some, and the first step in more fully integrating them is to develop your awareness. Understanding how lingering aspects of grandiosity are exhibited in a DNP can also help to understand why this person cannot recognize others as distinct and separate from them, and do not see them as worthwhile unique individuals.

CHARACTERISTICS OF LINGERING GRANDIOSITY

It can be difficult to draw a line between lingering aspects of infantile grandiosity, self-confidence, and self-esteem. We are each unique worthwhile individuals, and it is not grandiose to feel that way but is a vital component in healthy self-esteem. Many of us have also learned through experience and want to pass on our knowledge for others' benefit. Having aspirations to be successful and/or wealthy are not usually considered to be negative, nor is wanting to be important for others, such as children and family. The task becomes one of understanding how and when these thoughts, feelings, and attitudes are less components of appropriate self-confidence and self-esteem and more part of grandiosity. Read the following items and reflect on the extent to which these describe you, and if some of them seem to fit the person you think has a DNP. Rate yourself or the other person using the following scale: 1 — never or almost never; 2 — seldom or infrequently; 3 — sometimes; 4 — frequently; or 5 — always or almost always.

1. I daydream about being very successful and having others envy me.
2. I daydream about being very wealthy, what I would buy, and how others would envy me.
3. I feel I am essential to others' well-being and happiness.
4. I feel I make the difference for many things and many people.
5. I know what is best for others.
6. I tell others what they "should" do.
7. I remind others of what they "ought" to do.
8. Others do not perform to my level.
9. I put-down, or disparage, others.
10. I wish others would listen to me as I could prevent them from making mistakes.

Other examples of the lingering grandiosity are considering oneself to be more special than others, elite, more deserving of rewards and recognitions, not bound by the same rules as everyone else, and wanting to be envied. This is not an easy task, as we defend against awareness of our envy with rationalizations, displacement, and moral indignation.

There are some steps you can take to begin to understand any lingering aspects of grandiosity you may have and to distinguish grandiosity from confidence and self-esteem. One way of becoming aware of your own grandiose behavior, feelings, and attitudes is to examine how and for what you form judgments about others, your "shoulds and oughts," and what behaviors and attitudes of others trigger your anger. Your responses to these behaviors, feelings, and attitudes are indications of the degree of your sense of self-importance and entitlement. A sense of self-importance is not entirely negative. Self-esteem needs incorporate a feeling of being important, worthwhile, and unique, so we all have some degree of self-importance. When there is an inflated sense of self-importance, it is usually an indication of grandiose thinking and a feeling of being better than others, more worthy, and so forth.

Entitlement feelings, attitudes, and behaviors follow from grandiose positions. Entitlement is the demand that your needs justify any and all efforts by others to satisfy your needs, that they take precedence over others' needs, and that others are obliged to satisfy your needs. The demand may also be accompanied by insisting that others meet your needs without you having to tell them what they are.

Some indicators of lingering aspects of grandiosity are blaming, boasting, intolerance of criticism, and fantasizing being powerful, and so on.

BLAMING

Examine the extent to which you, or the person you think has a DNP, blame or judge others. Everyone judges others in some way. We form our opinions of others by making judgments about them based on our values. For example, if cleanliness is one of our values, we tend to make a negative judgement about people who are dirty or live in dirty surroundings. Another example is that we in the United States tend to judge veracity by the extent of wavering eye contact, and those who do not maintain eye contact are considered to be lying, sneaky, or sly. There are numerous examples of how we consciously and unconsciously make judgments about others. However, the extent to which our judgements and blame are ingrained, negative, and rigid may indicate some grandiosity.

Blaming is also a way of devaluing others. The end result is that the blamer can feel superior because he or she did not commit the act the other person did, or is not as inept or as incompetent. Others are seen as less worthwhile, making the blamer "perfect." Off-loading blame is putting the other person down and emphasizing his or her flaws.

BOASTING

Boasting can be seen as a form of the message "Look at me, now. Aren't I wonderful?" Feeling satisfaction about an achievement, overcoming a challenge, a difficult accomplishment, and other similar events is expected. The feelings of satisfaction are pleasant and contribute positively to our self-concept and our self-esteem. We can and do feel good about ourselves. There is also the urge to share this sense of satisfaction with others and the hope that they will feel a sense of pride and accomplishment with us. These are all expected feelings that any of us can identify with and probably have acted on. As described, this is not boasting.

Boasting occurs when someone not only feels a sense of satisfaction but also feels that whatever occurred proves their superiority, and is recounting accomplishments so that others will feel admiration and envy. The accomplishment is not enough; there must also be admiration and envy from others. Also, boasting can magnify an accomplishment out of proportion to its importance.

INTOLERANCE OF CRITICISM

An overreaction to or intolerance of criticism or of implied criticism is also indicative of grandiosity. The inflated sense of self-importance allows the DNP to assume that he or she is perfect and should not be criticized by anyone. Criticism is met with an attack, contempt, or disdain. The message is, "How dare you criticize me!" The destructive narcissist will react this way to implied criticism and tend to see remarks as criticism when that was not the intent.

Reflect on your reactions to criticism. Are you able to tolerate criticism from some people? Or does criticism make you feel as if you are being chastised or blamed? Do you feel flawed when criticized, as if you are so flawed that you will never overcome it? Is anger your immediate reaction to criticism?

If you have these or similar reactions to criticism, then you will want to practice stepping back cognitively when you are criticized and attempt to be somewhat objective. Being objective means that you can examine yourself, your actions, attitudes, and so forth, to see if there is any truth to the direct or implied criticism. You can ask if what you heard was what the other person said or meant, to determine if criticism was intended. It may not have been. Stepping back cognitively also allows you to distance yourself somewhat from your emotional response.

Being able to objectively observe yourself and the situation also allows you to be less focused on yourself and more aware of the other person. The person may not be accurate in their criticism, but something has triggered it. Observing allows you to understand whether the criticism is a projection, has some accuracy, or is being misunderstood. It takes distancing, but the outcome is that you become more tolerant of criticism and less reactive to it.

FANTASIZING POWER, WEALTH, AND SUCCESS

Daydreaming about winning the lottery, getting a promotion, having a hit record or book, becoming a movie star, or other kinds of achievements and successes can inspire children and adolescents to work harder to obtain their desires. Adults can have pleasurable moments fantasizing about the same kinds of things but get back to reality and either begin to work harder to achieve them, or accept and appreciate what they do have, or have been able to achieve. Lingering aspects of grandiosity may be indicated for adults when these dreams dominate much of their thinking and they feel that they have not been given what they deserve. The important concept is "given." The focus is not on the fact that they did not achieve these things, but on the notion that others did not make sure they received them.

GRANDIOSITY AND THE DNP

The destructive narcissist is driven by his or her fantasy of unlimited and unending wealth, success, beauty, brilliance, or of ideal love. Many or most of the actions of destructive narcissists are directed toward getting these things as their just rewards for being who they are. This is one of the reasons they pick up and discard people so easily. No one is able to give them what they feel they deserve, and so they move on to someone else. This new relationship is just as unsatisfying and unfulfilling as all the others, and so they continue to move on.

If you have had a relationship with a destructive narcissist, you may have encountered the following. At first the relationship runs smoothly. They are complimentary, seek your company, hang on to your words as if they are the greatest, and make you feel special. Gradually, or even suddenly, they begin to make disparaging remarks, become bored with you, tune out what you are saying, and make you feel inadequate. You may try harder to recapture the original specialness of the relationship, but your efforts are in vain. The harder you try, the more they pull away.

THE IMPOVERISHED SELF

Grandiosity also has another side, that of the impoverished self. The grandiose self is the inflated grand self whereas the impoverished self is the malnourished ineffective self. Both can exist in the same person, and are either firmly repressed or easily accessible. The latter state is the one that is seen in some destructive narcissists when you are interacting with his or her grandiose self, only to realize that he or she has changed to the impoverished self in a nanosecond. Others with a DNP only show the impoverished self to others, but the grandiose self lurks in the implications of their beliefs about themselves and the world. Examples of the dominance of the impoverished self with a lurking grandiose self can be seen in the following statements, especially if they are frequently heard from the same person.

"Things are stacked against me. If they were not, I would win, be a success,dominate, and so on."

"I never get the recognition I deserve" (or goods, services, encouragement, or admiration).

" I seem to always come in second-best."

"I don't know why I am in the fix I'm in."

How can you tell that there is lurking grandiosity and the person does not have low self-esteem? All the statements refer to external things or people, and not to a self-deficiency. For example, the first statement carries an implication that the speaker has the necessary ability, education, determination, and so on. It is only because of forces outside him or herself that produces the situation. Another clue to lurking grandiosity can be his or her response if or when you agree with their perceptions of inadequacy or of forces outside their control. When grandiosity is present, they will tend to respond as if you were criticizing them, or immediately switch to the obvious grandiose state, or dismiss your attempts to agree with them. You can end up puzzled or even upset about their responses to you.

Some people with a DNP display the impoverished self to certain people to gain their support, and generally get it. These supportive people do not see the lurking grandiosity, and can become very angry when others, who are presented primarily with the grandiose self, do not also agree with the perceptions of the supportive people, or give their support. This response or perspective only adds to your confusion at understanding what is happening and you can begin to question the validity of your perceptions and responses.

Once again, the destructive narcissist escapes self-responsibility, and others are left to deal with distressing feelings.

What has happened is that the destructive narcissist has projected his or her grandiose self onto you and was relating to you as if you were that ideal, grandiose, omniscient self. These people relate to you as they perceive themselves to be. When you disappoint them—and you cannot help doing so as you are not the projection—they devalue you as you really are. The destructive narcissist never saw you as a person, but only as an extension or projection of his or herself. No relationship can be maintained under these circumstances.

Another outcome of lingering aspects of grandiosity is the *lack of empathy*, the inability to sense the inner world of the other person and tune into another's feelings. Empathy implies an openness to others, an awareness of their separateness and individuality, and access to one's own spectrum of feelings. The impact of lack of empathy is discussed in the next section.

ADMIRATION NEEDS

ADMIRATION-SEEKING

Excessively seeking to be admired is a characteristic of some who have a destructive narcissistic pattern. These people can never receive enough approval and admiration, and will go to great lengths to achieve it, as they feel that admiration is to due them.

The need to be admired by everyone is, by definition, excessive. Almost everyone wants to be admired by others, but can be satisfied with receiving it from relatively few people. Most people do not have an expectation that they will be admired by everyone, nor do they demand or constantly seek admiration.

This chapter presents some behaviors and attitudes that are examples of how the needs for admiration and attention are exhibited. These needs may be age-appropriate, meaning that just because you do want to be admired or be the center of attention is not an indication of destructive narcissism as such, but is part of normal adult development. These needs are indicative of destructive or underdeveloped narcissism when they are intense and constant.

Admiration-seeking behavior is not necessarily destructive. It becomes destructive when combined with other characteristics, such as lack of empathy or concern for others, a devaluing of others, and grandiose, controlling behavior. Some admiration-seeking behaviors have more positive than negative

Table 4.1
Admiration-Seeking Behavior Scale (Reflect on the extent to which you or another person engages in each of these behaviors or attitudes)

---

1   Actively seeking the approval of others
2   Fishing for compliments or statements of recognition
3   Making sacrifices for others and making sure they are aware of it
4   Trying to be a superman or superwoman
5   Feeling dissatisfied with having less than the biggest or the best
6   Overspending or going in debt for obtaining unneeded material things and
        or services
7   Spending money to impress others
8   Gloating on winning
9   Flaunting or showing off possessions
10 Bragging about achievements, etc.
11 Wanting others to envy me

---

characteristics, but would still be classified as admiration-seeking behaviors because of the underlying need or motives.

Table 4.1 is a list of behaviors that can be classified as admiration-seeking when the conscious or unconscious motivation is to gain admiration from others. Complete the scale twice, once for the individual you have reason to believe may have a destructive narcissistic pattern and once to determine which of the behaviors and attitudes you possess.

Since it is almost impossible to know or be sure what our unconscious motivations are, the list should be answered as if your motivation was to secure admiration. That may or may not be the correct motive, but the intent of the list is to allow you to take an objective look at some of your behaviors and attitudes, to see whether you have a cluster of such behaviors that you engage in frequently or all the time. These behaviors and attitudes taken individually are not necessarily part of destructive narcissism. However, having a number of them that you frequently engage in may be part of a DNP.

POSITIVE ASPECTS OF ADMIRATION-SEEKING ATTITUDES AND BEHAVIORS

It is difficult sometimes to find positive aspects for many attitudes and be-haviors that fall into this category. It may also be difficult for individuals to be aware of their motives and accept that they are engaging in this behavior or that they have a particular attitude that has as its basis seeking admiration. Becoming aware of one's motivation is an important step in increasing one's awareness of admiration-seeking behaviors and attitudes. Following are some positive aspects or outcomes for these behaviors and attitudes.

SEEKING APPROVAL

This can be a form of "checking in" behavior to make sure the other person is getting his or her needs met, and that something is being done correctly, or that you are not going in the wrong direction. Asking, "Is this what you had in mind?" or "Is this supposed to be done this way?" or "Am I looking in the right place?" are examples of checking in. This is actively seeking reassurance but may also be a form of seeking approval. The same questions, when asked to manipulate others into giving praise or flattery, become admiration-seeking. Reassurance is not the same as approval, but it is easy to delude yourself into thinking that you are asking for reassurance when in reality you are asking for approval.

FISHING FOR COMPLIMENTS

This is a behavior that, if done infrequently, can have some positive aspects. It is more positive if done directly instead of through hints that one wants a compliment, etc., but there are times when the indirect approach may seem more appropriate to an individual. A positive aspect would be that you want to know that others noticed and are approving or pleased. For example, you may really want to know if the work you did on a committee was of value, and so you indirectly ask for recognition by asking someone, "I wonder if the committee work is noticed or acted on?"—expecting the response to be something like, "You are really doing a great job on the committee and I am sure the committee's work will be appreciated."

MAKING SACRIFICES

If you are inclined to sacrifice yourself for others and derive satisfaction from doing so, then this behavior is to be commended if not done to excess. It is seldom necessary to give up all of oneself for another person. The closest one can come to total sacrifice is in the care of children, the elderly, people who are ill , and so on., Sacrificing for a loved one in these circumstances is understandable. Almost all of us hope that care will be given to us if needed and that we will have the inner resources needed to give care to our loved ones if they should need it.

The kicker is the second part, making sure the recipients are aware of the sacrifice. Constantly or frequently bringing your sacrifice to their attention takes away from the positive aspect of giving and makes it closer to admiration-seeking behavior.

TRYING TO BE SUPERMAN OR SUPERWOMAN

There is a wonderful sense of accomplishment that can be felt when you are able to do many things and they all turn out well. The superpersons accomplish a great deal because they plan, organize, coordinate, and are able to move from one task to the other. They are also aware that life has many facets and work on being accomplished in most of them, that is, they are not narrow in focus. However, superpersons are prone to overextending their efforts and their relationships tend to suffer because they are constantly on the run. Their desire to do everything is fueled by others' admiration and not from an inner sense of satisfaction that comes from doing what one feels needs to be done for oneself or for others, such as family. The superperson is trying to satisfy his or her admiration needs.

DISSATISFACTION

Not settling for less than the best can inspire and encourage one to try harder to obtain it. Having the best of some things may be very important; for example, the best medical care for someone who is sick or injured, using the best materials for construction of a building or ship, having the best quality fruits and vegetables. The motive for having the biggest or best determines whether it is admiration-seeking behavior. If the dissatisfaction arises because of the internal desire to insure quality and not to arouse envy in others, then it can be very positive.

OVERSPENDING

There are occasions where it may be rewarding to overspend (but not overspend too much). Special events such as births, marriages, birthdays, anniversaries, graduation, a promotion, etc., call for some sort of recognition or celebration that may involve overspending. The key points for this kind of overspending are moderation and motive. Moderation means the amount of overspending is kept to the minimum needed to have a good time and meet the requirements of the situation. The motive for overspending is also very important. Is the motive to celebrate or is the motive to impress others? Putting on a lavish display to impress others is admiration-seeking behavior.

SPENDING TO IMPRESS OTHERS

Deliberately spending money in the effort to please others has no positive aspects. Examples include always picking up the check when dining out, buying a luxury car you cannot afford, or giving lavish presents. If, however, you do spend money without an intent to impress and the other person is impressed, then it is not termed admiration-seeking behavior.

GLOATING

There are no positive aspects to gloating.

SHOWING OFF

There are times when people show-off their possessions, such as a collection of antique cars, to share their uniqueness or the owner's caring for them. This sort of showing off is intended to allow others to see and share a common interest, not to arouse envy. Showing off collections can also be used as fund-raisers for charities. These are all positive aspects of showing off your possessions.

BRAGGING

There is a fine line between telling someone about a personal achievement or an accomplishment of self or others and bragging. There are no positive aspects of bragging.

WANTING OTHERS TO ENVY YOU

There are no positive aspects to this attitude.

NEGATIVE ASPECTS OF ADMIRATION-SEEKING BEHAVIORS AND ATTITUDES

Seeking admiration is an understandable behavior. We are social beings who want approval and appreciation. Wanting to be admired is not an unacceptable characteristic. However, constantly seeking and demanding admiration can be very wearing and have a negative impact on relationships, because this kind of admiration-seeking is usually accompanied by a devaluing or rejection of those who do not provide the needed admiration. Those who are not acceptably admiring are perceived as unworthy and are excluded.

It may be easy to see the negative aspects of the admiration-seeking behaviors in the scale, but the following discussion may present some aspects that are different. The negative aspects are based on the behavior or attitude being exhibited frequently or constantly.

SEEKING APPROVAL

Constantly needing the approval of others conveys an inadequate sense of self-confidence, self-efficacy, and/or self-esteem. The self-perception presented to others is a lack of inner security, self-understanding, and resources. Because the person does not have adequate resources and security from within, he or she seeks them from the external world. Having to constantly or frequently provide approval that most others can provide for themselves is tiring. It is not the case that anyone disapproves of their seeking approval, it is just that they get tired of always having to respond to this excessive and constant need for approval.

FISHING FOR COMPLIMENTS

The reaction to this form of admiration-seeking is similar to that for seeking approval from others. The behavior says, "Look at me and say how wonderful I am." Others will tend to view this as conceit and vanity carried to an extreme. Compliments and recognitions are very nice when freely given and not solicited. It is also easier to accept that they are sincerely meant when given spontaneously.

MAKING SACRIFICES

It is not difficult to appreciate the person who makes a sacrifice or sacrifices for you. Giving up something so that you benefit makes you feel cared for and valued, and you tend to return the feelings. However, when this appreciation is being constantly demanded, you get the feeling that the sacrifice is not to meet your needs but that you are being asked or required to meet the other person's needs. Most people react in a negative way to a frequent or constant demand for appreciation. Further, guilt feelings are aroused or imposed with these demands because the sacrificer is doing or giving something to the other person. Resentment on the part of both can be an outcome of this behavior.

TRYING TO BE SUPERMAN OR SUPERWOMAN

The most obvious negative aspect is that something important will not receive the needed attention. Important things include care of self, personal relationships, and personal growth, etc. There are only 24 hours in every day, and it is impossible to adequately attend to everything all the time. The negative outcomes of this behavior may not be readily apparent or emerge for a long time.

FEELING DISSATISFACTION

The feelings that are associated with having the biggest or best are fleeting, at best. There may be a glow of satisfaction, but it quickly dissipates and the dissatisfied feelings return. The dissatisfaction cannot be dispersed with material things; it comes from within. For this person, nothing is ever enough or is satisfactory except for fleeting moments. These feelings of dissatisfaction and the drive to fulfill the need to have the biggest or best can be very destructive to relationships.

OVERSPENDING

The desire to impress others with what one owns or is able to secure in services can cause overspending and considerable debt. Overspending and debt can lead to having inadequate money or credit for essentials, emergencies, or the ability to meet future needs. Impressing others is the goal, not having the goods or services.

SPENDING TO IMPRESS OTHERS

This behavior is similar to overspending in that both are done to impress others and thereby gain their admiration. Both entail overspending or going into debt but spending to impress assumes that the person is not going into debt but is spending lavishly to gain admiration from others, not because they want the goods or services. Leaving excessive tips, picking up the tab at dinner, taking everyone out to lunch, and giving expensive gifts are examples.

GLOATING

Gloating is reminiscent of childhood taunting behavior, and others react to it in much the same way: by being turned off. Being proud of winning or achieving is very different from gloating. Being proud is a personal affirmation of self without devaluing or disparaging the other person. Gloating means you are perceiving yourself as better and disparaging or putting down the other person. If you must gloat, do so in private.

SHOWING OFF

Constantly or frequently showing off your possessions is intended to arouse both envy and admiration. It also conveys an impoverished sense of inner self, as you want others to admire you for what you have, not who you are. The image others receive of you is what you present; it is based on your possessions, not how or what you really are. The flip side is that some may only judge you by your possessions and assume this is the real you. Flaunting is also a form of taunting.

BRAGGING

This form of admiration-seeking usually produces negative reactions from others. When you brag, others hear you as exaggerating your accomplishments, as being puffed up and conceited, and as putting down or ignoring the accomplishments of others. Bragging is a form of constantly promoting oneself at the expense of others.

WANTING OTHERS TO ENVY YOU

This occurs when it is not enough to feel good about yourself, your accomplishments, and your achievements; you also want others to admire you to the point where they not only want what you have, but are also intensely resentful of you. Envy is an eroding condition that has a very negative impact on the envious individual and on relationships. Envious people feel that they are more deserving than others and resent anyone who has what they want. The desire to have others feel this way about you is not conducive to building self-esteem or relationships.

DESTRUCTIVE ASPECTS OF ADMIRATION-SEEKING BEHAVIORS AND ATTITUDES

Constantly demanding admiration from everyone has a negative impact on relationships. People are picked up and discarded on the basis of how much and how well they can, or will, provide the needed admiration for the destructive narcissist. Because it is difficult to meet the need or demand for constant admiration, particularly when none is given in return, the destructive narcissist becomes dissatisfied with the relationship and starts looking for the next person who will meet that need. People are valued only to the extent to which they remain willing to meet these admiration-seeking needs.

Relationships are therefore transient and unsatisfying to those who have a DNP. They move from relationship to relationship ever seeking to fulfill the need for admiration. The discarded person in the relationship is often left puzzled and hurt at being abandoned, with little understanding of why he or she is being rejected. Some may even invest more of themselves in the relationship in an effort to maintain it but are usually not successful. The destructive narcissist cannot tell them what they want from them, that is, to always be admired and/or envied, as this need is on a nonconscious or unconscious level. Destructive narcissists are not aware that their need for admiration is excessive, deeply rooted, and demanding of others. They assume that everyone feels the same way and that because they are unique and special, they are entitled to have this need met.

SEEKING TO BE THE CENTER OF ATTENTION

Most people enjoy being the center of positive attention for brief periods. Positive attention can induce feelings of inclusion, acceptance, caring, approval, and so on. However, most people can accept that these are transient feelings when induced by outside events and seek to maintain these positive feelings based on inner experiencing. Few people will enjoy or seek to be the center of negative attention. Negative attention such as being questioned by the police, the media spotlight for an accusation of wrongdoing, making a fool of yourself in front of family and friends, getting stage fright to the extent that you cannot perform and having everyone look at you because you made a big mistake, are examples of negative attention that are not usually sought. However, there are some who will take attention any way they can get it—positive or negative.

Many people engage in attention-getting behaviors without being aware that this is what they are doing. Just because you may seek out and enjoy attention does not mean that it is part of a DNP. Wanting to be the center of attention is acceptable but can become a troublesome characteristic if many of the behaviors in the following scale are exhibited most or all the time.

The other considerations for deciding if the behaviors are attention-seeking are the motivation for the behavior and frequency with which they occur. Motivations for attention-seeking behavior may not be conscious, and for this reason are not identified as such by the person. That is, they may not be aware of why they engage in the behavior; nor do they see it as trying to be the center of attention.

Read the list of behaviors in the rating scale and be as objective as possible in estimating the frequency you engage in the particular behavior. After rating yourself, rate the individual you have reason to believe has a DNP.

CENTER OF ATTENTION RATING SCALE

1. Feeling that anything someone else can do, I can do better.
2. When talking to others, relating my activities with an attitude of "Can you top this?"
3. Teasing, using sarcasm, tickling, or holding something out of reach.
4. Making provocative remarks.
5. Losing my temper, or raising my voice.
6. Arriving late.
7. Pouting.
8. Sulking.
9. Withdrawing and hoping that others notice.
10. Waiting to be coaxed for participating.
11. Engaging in seductive behaviors.
12. Feeling jealous of attention given to others.
13. Making dramatic entrances and/or exits.
14. Talking loudly.

15. Nominating myself for awards or recognitions.

16. Joking even when it is not appropriate.

POSITIVE AND NEGATIVE ASPECTS OF ATTENTION-SEEKING CHARACTERISTICS

"ANYTHING YOU CAN DO, I CAN DO BETTER!"

Striving to improve performance or achievement is a positive characteristic. Using the level attained by others as a guide, being in competition, and wanting to do better are attributes that can encourage people to try harder and to extend themselves.

There are some negative aspects to this attitude and behavior. An intense competitive drive pushes individuals to strive harder against everyone, all the time. They can never be satisfied unless they best everyone else and may be ruthless in their quest to be better than anyone else all the time. They may also seek to devalue the accomplishments of others in the desire to be perceived as better.

"CAN YOU TOP THIS?"

Having a sense of pride about an accomplishment is laudatory, as is a friendly challenge to someone to try to do better. For example, many contributors to a charity, issue a challenge to encourage matching contributions from others. Individuals can set a performance standard and encourage others to match or exceed it.

Bragging is more than just being proud of something. It is an attitude that nothing or no one could possibly be better in any way. It can consist of taunting in order to make the other person appear to be inferior and to make oneself appear to be superior. Noting your accomplishments is positive; boasting and bragging are negative.

TEASING

Mild teasing of someone who is a friend and can accept it as such can strengthen a bond by providing shared laughter. Physical teasing, for example, tickling, as well as sarcastic teasing and continuous teasing are hurtful to the other person.

This is a way of demonstrating power and/or control over the other person. Physical teasing can be very demeaning to the other person. Acts such as snatching a hat and holding it out of reach, tickling, and ruffling hair are teasing behaviors. Sarcasm is a verbal form of teasing that can also be used for power and control. Engaging in these behaviors constantly, even with children, or especially with children, can be very demeaning and can amount to a show of power and control. After all, the other person is put in the position of appearing to be a poor sport if he or she complains or does not find the teasing funny.

MAKING PROVOCATIVE REMARKS

Although it may be more desirable to be direct, sometimes making a provocative remark can trigger a fruitful discussion about an important piece of information someone lacked or can lead people to begin to explore a new area of information.

This is another form of teasing. Dropping hints with no explanation, or refusing to explain or saying more, is a way of holding attention. Many may continue to mull over the remarks and assume that you know more than what you revealed. Motives for making provocative remarks may range from trying to impress others to making comments that can later be denied as having a particular meaning if necessary. These are the kind of comments that are open to different interpretations and the speaker can then change the intended meaning if it suits their purpose or need. This is an indirect and mostly dishonest way of communicating.

LOSING TEMPER, RAISING VOICE

There are very few times when it is positive to lose your temper. It usually does not help the situation or relationship. The only possible positive thing I can think of is that a display of temper adds emphasis to what you say and if you were not being listened to or taken seriously, raising your voice and letting your anger show may reverse those responses.

Loss of temper may get attention, but it is unlikely to command positive attention. It is more likely to be perceived as loss of control and to be reacted to in that way. When done on a consistent or regular basis, there is an indication of a more troubling underlying condition or problem.

ARRIVING LATE

Arriving late insures that others know you are attending. That may be important if attendance is encouraged or is mandatory. Another possible positive aspect of late arrival is not wasting time. Few events begin at the designated time, and arriving late means you do not have to sit or stand around waiting for things to get started.

Chronic lateness is annoying to others, as it can indicate indifference, resistance or reluctance, lack of organization, or the constant need for attention. Events and situations that make you late occasionally occur, and this can be understood and overlooked. However, if lateness is a pattern, then others may begin to perceive it as a deliberate act and react accordingly.

POUTING

No one is left in doubt about your feelings if you pout. You are being very direct in displaying your displeasure at not getting your way. The positive side is the openness and directness. There are more effective ways to do the same thing, but pouting is certainly one way to communicate your message.

Pouting is a childish response to not getting your way. It is an attempt to manipulate others by playing on their feelings. The child who pouts may become the center of attention, as adults want to please or make him or her feel better. Adults who pout are asking for the same thing and are sending the message that it is your or others' fault that they feel this way, and you are expected to take care of their feelings. It is surprising how often this behavior works. The dynamics of the relationship can often insure that the pouter will receive the needed attention and get his or her way in the effort to make him or her feel better.

SULKING

The sulker is verbally quiet about his or her anger, frustration, and hurt feelings, but is openly displaying them nonverbally. The person usually is silent; may withdraw physically; may exhibit suppressed feelings via posture, facial expression, and body positions; and may glare or stare to show displeasure. Like the pouter, one is seldom at a loss to know what the sulker is feeling. This is also an open expression of feelings.

Sulking, like pouting, is a childish response but with a different motive. The motive is more revenge than manipulation. By sulking, the individual is withdrawing his or her valuable self to punish others. The unspoken message is, "I will ignore you, not attend to you or your needs and make you regret what you did or said." All attempts by others to reconnect will be rebuffed. The sulker may receive the desired attention as more and more effort is expended by others in the attempt to placate him or her and to reestablish a relationship. However, over time, this behavior becomes less effective and others cease to try.

WITHDRAWING

There are situations that provoke intense affect where it may not be wise to allow the effect to be seen by the other person, for example, anger toward a supervisor or boss. These are the situations where it is wiser to withdraw than to stay. Another example is when conflict seems to be escalating. A temporary withdrawal allows intense affect to subside, and the conflict may be dealt with more constructively.

Withdrawing detaches you and builds a wall or moat between you and others. Running away or withdrawing is not conducive to maintaining relationships, as others cannot reach you. It can be a defensive, protective mechanism, but also works to keep others from making contact.

WAITING TO BE COAXED

Waiting for an invitation to join, participate, or be included can give some assurance that one's presence is desired. It is not a pleasant feeling to realize that one's presence is only being tolerated or is being rejected, and there are circumstances where it may be better to wait for an invitation rather than intruding. This, of course, assumes that waiting to be coaxed is not a pattern of behavior but is unique to the particular situation.

Others will become weary and be turned off if the usual behavior is waiting to be coaxed. How many times must one be encouraged and assured for the person to feel secure enough to take responsibility?

ENGAGING IN SEDUCTIVE BEHAVIOR

Mild flirting under certain conditions can be fun. It is playful and harmless if both parties have the same understanding that they are just playing. However, other kinds of seductive behavior can be distressing to other people and it may be better to avoid them. Behaviors like pouting, sulking, withdrawing, and waiting to be coaxed can also be classified as seductive.

Seductive behaviors are used to manipulate responses from others. The seducer wants something but does not ask for it in a direct and open manner leading to the other person feeling manipulated and used. In some ways it shows contempt for the other person, the implication being that the person can be controlled and made to do something he or she would not otherwise do.

Feeling Jealous of Attention Given to Others

Jealousy has no positive aspects. It is a feeling that one is not getting what one deserves, and attention is being unfairly given to another person who is undeserving. Wanting some attention is very different from being jealous that someone felt to be less worthy is getting the attention.

Attention-getting behavior as a result of jealousy is usually very evident to everyone. Jealousy results from a profound feeling of being abandoned and forsaken by the loved one for someone else who is deemed to be less worthy. The jealous person portrays his or her longing for the person, anger at him or her for the perceived faithlessness, and contempt for the person receiving the attention. A very unlovely picture.

Making Entrances or Exits

A dramatic or attention-getting entrance or exit can add a dash of excitement and interest to an event. If this is a seldom-used behavior, it can be pleasurable to both participant and observer. An exit can highlight leave-taking, thereby giving all an opportunity to say goodbye.

Constantly disrupting the proceedings becomes annoying and distasteful to others as time goes on. Too many dramatics lessen the impact, leading to increasingly outrageous behavior or sulking. Judicious and intermittent use of this tactic can keep its effectiveness, but too much is a definite turnoff.

Talking Loudly

Sometimes you have to talk loudly to be heard. It can also be helpful in gaining the attention of someone who may not be alert to a potential accident, for example, a red light at a busy intersection. Instructors and presenters need to talk loudly so that they can be heard by all.

People do tend to become annoyed at those who talk loudly because it is disruptive and intrusive. Further, people who talk loudly also tend to talk a lot, talk constantly, and interrupt others. Talking loudly can produce in others feelings of being overwhelmed and controlled, leading to feelings of discomfort and leading to avoidance behavior. If you tend to talk loudly, you may be surprised at the number of people who long to tell you to "be quiet" or "shut up!"

Nominating Yourself

There are awards and recognitions that encourage self-nominations and this maybe the only way that anyone knows of your interest and/or accomplishments. Waiting for others to recognize your achievements and make a nomination is not always productive. There are many organizations that are so large that it is difficult for all individuals to be known well, and self-nominations are one way to find qualified individuals who may otherwise be overlooked.

Putting yourself out front of everyone else conveys arrogance to many. The idea that you consider yourself to be better goes against many cultural values of waiting to be recognized. Further, you may not get or be able to muster support for the nomination, leading to possible feelings of resentment and alienation.

Joking

Everyone likes to laugh, and having a sense of humor can help keep things in perspective. The ability to see humor and absurdities is a characteristic to be cultivated. Laughter is fun, makes people feel good, can strengthen relationships, and can be healing. Joking can be healing and is a very positive characteristic.

It is very easy to tell jokes that are offensive to some segment of the population-even if you yourself are a member of the particular segment. The attitude that others should have a sense of honor, that you did not mean anything derogatory, or that others should not be so sensitive tends to beg the question. Whether intended or not, jokes have a great potential to offend. Joking also keeps others at a distance and carries the threat of making them the target or brunt of your humor.

SUMMARY

The behaviors and attitudes described are only examples for admiration- and attention-seeking. These are but a few of many that can be exhibited by the destructive narcissist. You may have found that you too engage in some of the behaviors and attitudes, but tend to do so to a lesser extent. The destructive narcissist constantly engages in admiration- and attention-seeking behaviors and does not understand that this is what they are doing, and is indifferent to the impact of their needs for admiration and attention. They go from person to person in search of someone who can supply them with constant unconditional admiration and attention and are profoundly disappointed when no one can adequately meet these needs.

CHAPTER 5

Troubling States: Emotions, Emptiness, and Entitlement

The behaviors and attitudes discussed in this chapter are inner states that are generally inferred from behaviors, attitudes, and the impact these have on others, rather than being directly observed. The ones discussed are shallow emotions, emptiness, and entitlement. These can be troubling both to the person experiencing them, to others in their relationships, or for those who have to interact with them on a regular basis. These states can be troubling to the person who has them because they sense that others have something they do not, even when they cannot identify what that something is. The states are troubling to others because they expect a higher level of development for these adults, and react to them on the basis of these flawed expectations. Indeed, these expectations may not be conscious, but they do react to others as if they experience a wide range and depth of emotions. It can be upsetting, disconcerting, and infuriating at times to realize that someone is less developed than you thought—has shallow emotions.

SHALLOW EMOTIONS

Most adult humans experience a wide variety of emotions and can express themselves. Most are able to experience a range of intensity for emotions from very mild, such as annoyance, to very intense, such as rage. Even those who substitute rational thoughts for feelings have the capacity to experience many emotions.

Destructive narcissists are characterized by their shallow emotional life. They do not have the capacity to experience a wide variety or depth of emotions. They use the correct words to describe an emotion but do not convey the affect connected with it. This seems to hold true for emotions, with the exceptions of anger and rage. Usually no one is unclear about destructive narcissists' feelings when they are angry or enraged, but you may receive mixed messages about other emotions. For example, a destructive narcissist may say he or she is sad about a spouse being sick, but what they convey is that they feel resentment (i.e., anger) at having their plans disrupted.

Matt stunned the department at its monthly meeting by announcing that he and his wife of many years were getting a divorce. The reasons people were stunned were many; he announced it as he entered the room which interrupted the proceedings. Everyone else mostly did not talk about their personal lives or concerns at department meetings so his action was unusual, and they were presented with a dilemma on whether to ignore the announcement or to stop what they were doing and respond. Some people expressed sadness about the breakup, and Matt responded that his wife was more upset than he was. They found out the next week that Matt was entering a cohabitation arrangement with another woman, Goldie.

Matt and Goldie did live together for about three years although she took a job in another city some distance from Matt. Prior to her taking the job, they had a child though in vitro fertilization. Matt commuted every week from there to the city where he worked. Goldie and Matt finally moved to the city where he worked and she found employment there. However, not long after they moved, they broke up. She took the child and moved to another state. Matt's coworkers thought that he would be depressed and sad. But, Matt was cheerful, although he said that he was sad. He laughed often, sought social interactions, cracked jokes, walked briskly, and showed no signs of depression or sadness. He also immediately started a relationship with another woman.

There are many life experiences that can produce intense and deep emotions, but most people share these experiences with the people who are near and dear to them, not just anyone. Shared with the bulk of casual and work acquaintances are general events that do not carry intense or deep emotions. You generally select the people with whom you share your intimate feelings and experiences.

What Matt did was a demonstration of the shallowness of his emotions, flitting from relationship to relationship without seeming to have deep and passionate caring. The breakup of a cherished and valued relationship produces considerable grief and sadness that is not easily concealed. Even if you laugh, while inside you are crying cannot be completely, concealed all the time. It's too hard to preserve that facade. One other way destructive narcissists demonstrate a shallow emotional life is through their inability to tolerate others' intense emotions. You and others may find it uncomfortable to experience someone's intense emotions, especially negative feelings such as sadness, and use a variety of means to avoid people who are experiencing negative emotions. There are also times when you avoid such people because you may be caught up in your own problems and feel you do not have the energy to deal with others' feelings. However, in both instances, you are usually aware of what you are doing even if you do not know why you are doing it. Destructive narcissists have no awareness that they are unable to tolerate others' intense emotions and are avoiding expressions of emotion, and if this behavior was pointed out to them, would have no concept of what they were doing. This holds true for intense positive emotions, such as happiness, as well as more negative ones, such as sadness.

Consider what it is like to feel neither joy nor despair. Both are intense, peak experiences, and while despair is uncomfortable, the ability to feel it enriches us and contributes to understanding the human condition. The capacity for a rich, varied, and intense emotional life is part of a well-integrated personality and necessary for satisfying, meaningful relationships. The ability to experience and appropriately express emotions contributes to intimacy in relationships. The following discussion highlights some ways in which the shallow emotional life of a destructive narcissist impacts development and maintenance of satisfying relationships.

EMOTIONAL INTIMACY

There are different kinds of intimacy: physical intimacy, which involves touching, caressing, hugging, holding, and sexual expression; cognitive intimacy, which involves sharing ideas, and emotional intimacy, which involves the sharing of deepest feelings directly and openly. The destructive narcissist has poor intimate relationships. He or she may have many partners but lack emotional intimacy with any of them. Physical intimacy may not be a problem, but emotional intimacy is out of the DNP's reach.

Emotional intimacy occurs when we are willing to risk letting other persons experience us as we really are in the hope and expectation that they can accept us and, in return, risk showing us themselves as they really are. We seek to be loved, appreciated, and cared for. This definition of emotional intimacy makes it easy to see why destructive narcissists do not have the capacity for emotional intimacy. They do not appreciate others as separate, worthwhile, and unique individuals; rather, they see others as extensions of self and/or devalue them. They do not love others, as they only want others to love them without anything given in return or expected of them. They do not care for others as they feel they are entitled to be cared for, lack empathy with others, and consider themselves to be unique and special.

This inability to have emotional intimacy is part of the reason they have many partners. These are the people who marry many times (three or more) due to divorce. There may be other contributing causes for the breakups, such as alcoholism or abuse, but their pattern is to pick up and discard relationships over and over. The number of marriages does not begin to convey the number of relationships they have had over their lifetime. The pattern is an inability to form and maintain meaningful relationships.

DEVELOPMENT OF CAPACITY FOR EMOTIONAL INTIMACY

The development of the capacity for emotional intimacy moves through stages that parallel expected human growth and development. The stages may overlap, and individuals may become stuck in a stage and the quality of their emotional intimacy in relationships affected. The stages are (1) self-centered; (2) idealized image; (3) reflection of a projected self; (4) awareness of being separate; and (5) mutuality. This discussion focuses on describing the stages with emphasis on the destructive nature of some behaviors and attitudes that impact relationships. You may find that the person you have in mind, or even yourself, are stuck in an earlier stage, and expectations for the degree of emotional intimacy are not realistic.

SELF-CENTERED STAGE

Emotional intimacy is not possible in this stage because there is only taking, with no giving in return. Emphasis is on having one's needs gratified, and others are valued only to the extent to which they can meet these needs. Physical satisfactions are the primary sources of feelings for another person, but if that person wants emotional intimacy along with physical intimacy, he or she is quickly discarded.

There is also an element of possessiveness in self-centered emotional intimacy development. The other person is to be controlled and must not exercise any initiative or self-determination. The other's reason for existing is to meet needs, and the person in this stage can be very demanding, clinging, and possessive. Adults in this stage cannot be mutually intimate, they can only take from others.

It is easy to understand that infants and children begin at this stage. Their needs are the most important thing in their world, and to them others exist to meet these needs, as the very young are incapable of meeting them for themselves. The infant misses the person who satisfies his or her needs and becomes very frustrated and angry when the person is not available. This is not so easy to understand in adults where the expectation is that they will be more developed and not perceive others as extensions of self.

Some destructive narcissists appear to function at this stage of emotional intimacy. They have numerous partners, marry, and divorce often, and appear to select friends and partners on the basis of what others can give or provide that meets the destructive narcissist's needs with no reciprocity.

IDEALIZED IMAGE STAGE

In this stage others are related to in terms of how well they meet an idealized image. The ideal is developed from an internal image of the satisfying other. The relationship is still based on having needs met, but there is some awareness of the other person as being separate and distinct.

Relationships for this stage are developed on the unconscious basis of "like me-not like me" or "this is how I see myself." Differences are minimized or ignored and the other is related to as if he or she were the self. Another aspect is that the other is perceived only in positive ways and everything is positive. The messages are "He or she is wonderful!" therefore "I am wonderful!" The inability to integrate polarities and accept both positive and negative aspects of self and others has a significant impact on relationships.

This stage seems to parallel psychological development, where the child begins to separate and individuate, to see self as separate and distinct from others, and to recognize their individuality. Others may still be related to as extensions of self, but not as totally so as in the previous stage. This stage spans many years in psychological development, and there are levels of development within the stage.

The ability to integrate polarities about self and others also occurs during this stage and is progressive. Self and others are not always perceived as all good or all bad (dualistic thinking), but the polarities are integrated so that there need not be total acceptance or total rejection.

Emotional intimacy is less demanding at this stage. Absences of the other can be better tolerated, and the person can engage in self-directed behavior and initiatives. The destructive narcissist, however, can remain stuck at the beginning levels of this stage and still relate to others with little integration of polarities and scant recognition of others as separate and distinct individuals. Some may be at a higher level in the stage, but may not have completed the growth and development of the capacity for emotional intimacy. Others are still perceived and related to in terms of self, and there is little or no success in forming and maintaining satisfying intimate relationships. As soon as the other person exhibits any behavior less than ideal, the relationship begins to deteriorate and is soon terminated.

REFLECTIONS OF A PROJECTED SELF STAGE

This may not be a separate stage but may describe the highest level of the previous stage. However, it does describe an individual who has more capacity for emotional intimacy than does the person in the idealized stage. Polarities are better integrated and others are not expected to be totally good or totally bad; they can be accepted as having a small degree of both polarities.

Others are related to and valued to the degree that they reflect expectations or perceptions of self. Projections of parts of self can occur, and others are related to via these projections. Others are not seen as they are, and must reflect this perception if there is to be a relationship—whether or not the perception of the characteristic is accurate or not.

This stage also has elements of the self-centered stage, where others have value only to the degree that they can meet needs, and are extensions of self. This characteristic differs significantly in this stage in degree and intensity. The individual in this stage has less of a need to have others meet some of their own needs and some ability to accommodate the needs of others. However, others are expected to meet their needs to a significant extent and to be controlled.

AWARENESS OF BEING SEPARATE STAGE

The awareness stage occurs when the individual can perceive himself or herself as separate and distinct from others in most ways, can perceive others as different, and can tolerate these differences. Others are valued as worthwhile, unique individuals as well as self, and are not expected only to serve the self.

This stage is characterized by a considerable integration of polarities where the individual can accept both positive and negative characteristics of himself or herself and of others. Others are not all good or all bad, and it becomes possible to separate actions from being.

The destructive narcissist does not adequately develop to fully enter this stage, which is characterized by the ability to form and maintain lasting, meaningful relationships; where individuals can be prized, cherished, and accepted as they are; and where one can be interdependent as well as independent. The perception of others as extensions of self in many ways continues to prevent the destructive narcissist from this stage of emotional intimacy.

MUTUALITY STAGE

This stage is characterized by a capacity for deep, intimate relationships. Individuals accept themselves as they are and can accept others as they are. They are capable of sustained empathy, and can experience and exhibit a wide range of human emotions. The inability to experience or access deeper emotions can be a reflection of the destructive narcissist's emptiness at the core of him or herself. This is the focus for the next discussion.

EMPTINESS

To visualize the terrors of emptiness, picture yourself in outer space. There is no up or down, no familiar landmarks; you are floating secure in your space suit but realize that there is no air available except the little you carry and there is no spaceship for safety. As you look around, you see nothing, and while you know you are floating in the absence of gravity, you feel as if you are falling and it is dark and cold. You cannot orient yourself because there is nothing. You cannot direct your movements; nor do you have any sense of where you could move to be safe. There is nothing—no human contact, no familiar things such as a sun or horizon, no direction, no stability, and no noise, nothing—just the vast, seemingly endless, empty universe.

The terror occurs because there is no way to know who or where one is, to be safe, or to control events in any way. Even a hole is defined by its surroundings, no matter how large it may be. Emptiness has no defining parameters and, for that reason, is terrifying. Humans seem to work hard to avoid experiencing this terror, and this is understandable. However, the core of oneself contains the personhood of many people, and is a source of guidance, confidence, creativity, and meaning. The core of this self is not empty, and one doesn't have to fear accessing that core, as does the destructive narcissist, because that core keeps you centered and grounded, and sustains your ability to make meaningful contact with others, and to have meaning and purpose for your life.

Emptiness is also difficult to define because it can only be described in comparison with the presence of something. Related terms used include void, space, and vacuum. Synonyms are hollow, unfilled, unfurnished, unoccupied, vacant, barren, bare, fruitless, and meaningless. All these concepts are understood as contrasting with the presence of something.

Further complicating matters, other terms and concepts are sometimes used interchangeably with "emptiness." Terms and concepts such as loneliness, numbness, and depression are often what is meant when people say they are empty. In this discussion of the DNP, emptiness is considered to be very different from loneliness, numbness, and depression.

LONELINESS VERSUS EMPTINESS

Loneliness can be characterized by an absence of meaningful human relationships together with a longing and yearning for them. There is also an awareness and knowledge of what it feels like not to be lonely, to be connected in a significant way.

A lonely person can feel pain, especially pain around lack of a meaningful relationship. While pastimes and other activities may be used to deal with or mask the pain, the person can readily access the pain. It is suppressed, not repressed or denied.

Another characteristic that distinguishes loneliness from emptiness is the ability to experience a wide range of emotions and to experience intense emotions. These can be negative, such as rejection and dejection, or positive, such as satisfaction or pleasure. Individuals may be lonely but have not cut off their ability to experience emotions.

The emptiness experienced in the DNP differs from loneliness in all these aspects. Destructive narcissists have not been able to establish meaningful relationships and, although they may wish for one at a deep level, there is no awareness or knowledge of what a meaningful relationship is like. They do not know what it means to be connected in a meaningful way.

The unwillingness and/or inability to allow themselves to feel pain around absence of a meaningful relationship also distinguishes a DNP. This is very difficult to describe, as it seems incredible that one cannot feel the pain of loneliness, that is, the lack of a meaningful relationship. Rationalizing not having one or choosing to isolate oneself because of hurtful and unsatisfying past relationships can be understood. But not feeling the pain associated with loneliness is difficult to understand and accept. One reason the destructive narcissist is able to manipulate others is that we erroneously assume that the destructive narcissist experiences emotions as we and others do. The destructive narcissist does not.

Closely tied to absence of pain is the destructive narcissist's inability to experience a wide range of emotions and to experience any intense emotion other than anger. I generally describe the destructive narcissist's range of emotion as being from A to B, with all the intensity of a dewdrop. Just think of what it might be like not to experience joy or grief. While it is uncomfortable and may even be undesirable to experience certain emotions, such as despair, our ability to do so also tells us we have the capacity to experience more positive ones, such as joy.

NUMBNESS VERSUS EMPTINESS

Grief and shock can produce a feeling of numbness. This may seem like a contradiction because being numb usually means not feeling anything, but this is somewhat different in that you are aware of feeling numb. There is a heaviness connected to numbness, a deadening of the pain. The numbness protects you from feeling pain.

Numbness is not emptiness because it is temporary, an unusual state, you know what "should" or could be felt and you have experienced a wide range and intensity of emotions prior to becoming numb. You may even fear the loss of numbness because you know there is pain behind it.

Grief or shock over the loss of a loved one indicates a capacity for forming a meaningful relationship, especially when the lost relationship was a mutual one. Grieving is a process that usually begins with being numb, and while grieving can occur with any loss, this discussion focuses on grief around a relationship and the accompanying feeling of numbness.

Numbness is described as the absence of feeling. If asked to say what is felt, most would reply, "Nothing." It is not a denial of feeling, but rather an absence of feeling. The person knows what it feels like to experience an emotion, such as relief or anger, and also knows when there is nothing there. There may also be a cognitive awareness that the numbness will not last and that the resulting flood of emotions the numbness has dammed will be intense. However, the dread is not felt, but only thought about.

DEPRESSION VERSUS EMPTINESS

Feeling blue, down in the dumps, or depressed is not emptiness. Even diagnosed clinical or major depression, a more intense depression, is different from emptiness. Depression is accompanied by feelings that range from mild to intense. These feelings, although negative, provide something, whereas in emptiness there is nothing.

Some feelings that accompany depression are worthlessness, hopelessness, helplessness, despair, and meaninglessness. Depressed people focus on and magnify their faults and berate themselves as having little or no value. They may obsess over minor errors and make them into larger mistakes than they really are.

Another feeling is hopelessness. They lack hope that either they or their circumstances will change for the better. They also feel it is hopeless to expect that they could do anything to change their circumstances for the better. Along with hopelessness is the feeling of helplessness. They neither hope to change nor feel competent to effect change that will be better. They feel helpless to prevent distressing circumstances or to have any effect. They neither expect to do something nor expect that any actions taken will have positive outcomes.

Despair occurs when all avenues appear to be blocked and one remains mired in misery. There may be a longing and yearning for meaningful contact with others but no real hope that it is possible to make these connections. No efforts are made because there is no hope of success, and so the downward spiral accelerates into deeper and deeper despair. The despairing person cares very deeply and is hurt and angry about being what he or she perceives as ineffectual in preventing harm to self and others. Such a person cannot keep others, or self, from frustration, failure, rejection, etc., leading to feelings of worthlessness, hopelessness, helplessness, and despair.

As you can see, the depressed person is full of feelings, usually intense, and knows the experience of meaningful contact with others. He or she is not empty.

EMPTINESS AND THE DNP

Emptiness for someone who has a DNP includes strong feelings of boredom, repressed or suppressed hostility, and restlessness, coupled with a lack of capacity for forming and maintaining meaningful relationships. Many people may have periods where they feel bored and restless, experience a loss of direction or purpose, or lack a meaningful relationship. However, this is transitory and is not a consistent pattern in their lives, especially the capacity to form and maintain meaningful relationships. The destructive narcissist lacks this capacity.

Emptiness is a void, nothing, and the destructive narcissist, like many others, seeks to escape emptiness through activity. Examples are many social activities, drugs, alcohol, sex, food, aggression, or other compulsive activities that reduce or preclude opportunities for inner reflection. When you are busy, you do not have to experience emptiness. However, the strong component of boredom and restlessness pushes the destructive narcissist to more and more intensity and/or activities. Activities, like people, lose their novelty and appeal for the destructive narcissist, and the person must keep moving in order to avoid experiencing emptiness.

This emptiness seems endless, but experienced therapists propose that the emptiness defends against depression, with all the feelings it contains, and despair. On the other side of emptiness is depression, despair, fear of destruction, and fear of abandonment. One has to work through these feelings and fears in order to come to joy, purpose, meaning, and connectedness. The destructive narcissist so fears experiencing the terrors of emptiness and the downward spiral of depression with all its hopelessness, helplessness, despair, and fears of destruction and abandonment that he or she constantly defends against it and keeps moving. This has been a pattern since early years, and the destructive narcissist cannot conceive of any other way of being.

ENTITLEMENT

The destructive narcissist has a deep sense of entitlement. This sense of entitlement contributes to much of the frustration felt by others who interact with him or her. However, almost everyone has some sense of entitlement, and one way to understand the DNP is to become aware of just how you manifest your sense of entitlement.

The conscious or unconscious assumption that one's needs could and should be met without any effort on their part is a definition of entitlement. The underlying basis for the assumption is that the person is so unique and special that he or she deserves to do whatever he or she wants to, whenever he or she desires, and others exist to serve their needs and desires. While this may seem somewhat extreme and not descriptive of you at all, you may find that you do exhibit some level of the entitlement assumption in some area of your life.

For example, do any of the following describe your behavior or attitudes? If so, then this is an aspect of entitlement you display.

- Things should always be done exactly as you want them done.
- Others should anticipate your needs and meet them.
- Others are to blame when your needs or wants are not met.

- Others are expected to show concern with none shown in return.
- You expect preferential treatment.
- Others must be sympathetic or empathetic toward you.
- Others should do things or give gifts to show that they care for you.
- Others should always be sensitive to your moods, feelings, etc.
- Others should put your needs before theirs.
- You expect to be in charge.
- You expect others always to agree with you.
- You expect to get all rewards and recognitions.
- You do not expect any consequences for breaking rules or laws.

The statement *"Do things my way"* is an example of an attitude and behavior that can illustrate entitlement. While it is also indicative of control issues, the conscious or unconscious assumptions are that you know best and others must recognize that and carry out your wishes. You feel you have the knowledge of how things must be done and it is imperative that others make sure things are done this way. For example, it is not good enough for someone simply to clean his or her desk; the work must be your version of clean and organized.

Reflect on the following attitudes, feelings, and behaviors and ask yourself if any are descriptive of you. The phrasing may not be entirely accurate, but may come close to describing your experience. Do you, most of the time, feel uncomfortable or anxious when things do not appear to you to be in order; when others do things their way, which appears inefficient and/or ineffective; when you have specified how you want something done and others do not do it this way? Do you demand that the task be redone to your satisfaction?

This can signal your need to have things done your way. Destructive narcissists may be extreme in demands that everything be done their way, but many others have this behavior and attitude in common with them.

"Give it to me before I have to ask" reflects an attitude that exemplifies expecting others to meet your needs without your having to tell them to do so. This may be especially frustrating to others when coupled with the attitude "I should not have to tell you; you should know." This attitude is understandable in an infant and child. They cannot fend for themselves nor are they able to adequately communicate their needs. Infants and children are, however, able to communicate their displeasure and frustration, in unmistakable terms, at not having their needs met.

Reflective of this characteristic of entitlement for adults are attitudes and feelings such as disappointment when you do not get the gift you wanted even though you were asked what you would like and did not tell the person, maybe even saying, "Anything would be okay." Another example is expecting your spouse to intuit what you want him or her to do or say. While a destructive narcissist expects others to always anticipate his or her needs and desires and fulfill them, some others have a less demanding form of this characteristic.

Blaming others when your needs are not met is related to the previous characteristic. The destructive narcissist is quick to off-load any hint that he or she is not perfect, and whatever happens is warped around to being your, or someone's fault. A part of blaming is the feeling of entitlement. Destructive narcissists consider themselves entitled to have others insure that they succeed at everything, and if there is any failure, then it is someone else's fault and they are not to blame.

Even those who do not have a destructive narcissistic pattern may find themselves tending to blame others when things do not go as they wish. Blame is different from understanding and ascribing causes for an outcome. Understanding what mistakes were made so that they can be corrected is not blaming. Blame carries with it the suggestion that the person should not have done what was done and should be ashamed, or that the person is fatally flawed. There is a strong component of shame or shaming attached to blame.

Destructive narcissists fool many people for a long time because everyone wants to accept that they are genuine in their expressions of concern for others. They use the words but do not have the meanings or feelings to go along with the words. It is only after some time that you begin to realize that there has been *no concern shown for you, or for others*. Sometimes the realization occurs in response to some event, such as illness.

One example of a real event that illustrates this characteristic happened to a secretary.

She had to have an operation for carpal tunnel syndrome on her right arm and hand. She was right-handed and was supposed to limit use of the arm and hand after the operation. Her boss expressed concern about her condition and the need to have an operation, saying that he or she would assist in any way and that the boss was sure others in the office would also assist. However, the day before the operation, her boss asked her how long she planned to be out, even though all this had been previously discussed. When the secretary said that the surgeon recommended that she stay home one week, the boss said that was too long. The boss also asked how long it would before she, the secretary, would be able to write and was told it would be two to three weeks. The boss said then that two to three weeks was too long and it was necessary for her to write much sooner. This is the same boss who expected everyone to show concern about the magnitude of the job, every little and big problem that emerged, and every personal ache and pain.

Being unique and special also means that *preferential treatment* is expected. Destructive narcissists assume that they will receive preferential treatment and become very angry when they do not. Their needs and desires, spoken and unspoken, come before anyone else's and must be attended to. There will also be some anger and envy around preferential treatment shown to others.

It can be very pleasant to receive preferential treatment sometimes. Getting a good table in a restaurant, not having to wait in line, having your name placed at the top of the list are examples of preferential treatment that can make you feel good. You did not have to do anything to receive preference; it just came.

I remember an incident that made me feel special because I received preferential treatment. My luggage did not get on the plane with me and arrived on a later flight. Someone from the airline called and said my luggage was in and would be delivered to my home. I asked if he could estimate the time of day, for example, afternoon, and was told he could not as there were many deliveries all over the region. I shrugged to myself and said that would be okay. I was pleased the luggage had arrived and had no pressing need for it. Imagine my surprise when about twenty minutes later the doorbell rang and a man stood there with my luggage. I expressed surprise that it arrived so soon, and he said he put me at the top of the list because I was nice on the phone. A destructive narcissist would have assumed that he or she would automatically be first on the list and be very angry if he or she were told anything different.

Entitlement of *sympathy and empathy* is related to showing concern. Almost everyone appreciates receiving sympathy and empathy at needed times. They reduce isolation and loneliness and promote connectedness with others. However, expecting others to meet these needs assumes that you are entitled to have them met. The attitude of the destructive narcissist is that others are not expected to freely give sympathy and empathy; rather, others are expected to provide them because the destructive narcissist deserves them, that is, is entitled to them.

Even if you are not a destructive narcissist, you may exhibit a milder form of the entitlement attitude. This attitude is one that may be on a nonconscious or unconscious level, that is, below your awareness. Ask yourself if you become disappointed, depressed, or angry when you do not receive expected sympathy or empathy. When undergoing distress, do you expect everyone to sympathize and/or empathize with you? If so, then there is some measure of entitlement present.

Recognizing this attitude in a destructive narcissist occurs over time. If you show sympathy or empathy appropriately to him or her, you will be expected to express sympathy and empathy for everything that happens to that person, be fully with the destructive narcissist at all times because he or she is deserving. Slowly, you become aware of how often you are expressing sympathy or empathy and the fact that none is shown to you in return.

Ways of showing that you care for or love someone include *giving gifts*, doing things for the person that are intended to please, increase the person's comfort, or decrease discomfort. We all like to be cared for and receive love from a loved one. However, we usually are somewhat uncomfortable receiving symbols of care or love from those we do not care for in the same way as their actions and gifts indicate they care for us. Destructive narcissists, on the other hand, expect everyone to do things for them, give them gifts, they and do not feel uncomfortable in receiving these without returning the affection.

A check on your attitude about gifts and actions of others is to ask yourself if you feel disappointed when coworkers, friends, and others do not remember your birthday or other special events. Are you disappointed when others do not do favors for you or anticipate what you need to have done and do it? The difference between anticipation of gifts and favors and feeling entitled to them is in level and intensity. Becoming pleased or happy at receiving gifts and favors without being disappointed if they are not forthcoming indicates a healthy response. Being angry and/or disappointed at not receiving gifts and favors from many people indicates more of an entitlement attitude.

Everyone, at some time, can appreciate someone being *sensitive to his or her mood*. When you are sad or blue, it helps if someone asks if he or she can be of assistance by listening. When you are happy, it is nice to have someone recognize your happiness and want to share it. However, most of us do not expect people to be paying such close attention to us that they know and respond to our every mood. Having attentive parents in childhood who were sensitive to our moods contributed to a feeling of security and self-esteem, but adults do not expect other adults to be as responsive. Adults can be characterized as having some self-sufficiency and the ability to accept responsibility for their moods.

Destructive narcissists have an assumption that others are supposed to be in tune to their moods and cater to their needs. You are supposed to intuit what they are feeling without being told. In some instances, destructive narcissists may also blame you for their moods, but interestingly, you never get credit for producing a "good" mood.

Destructive narcissists expect their *needs to receive priority*. They assume that whatever they need is much more important than what you need and you should be willing to delay getting your needs met until theirs have been met. Remember, what most may consider a desire or want, the destructive narcissist is likely to consider a need. So, even if the "need" appears to you to be a desire, to the destructive narcissist it is a need.

Parents generally put their children's needs before their own. Mature adults are characterized by the ability to delay gratification, whereas immature adults and children are not able to delay gratification. They want what they want, and they want it now. One measure of how you stand with respect to needs priorities is your ability to delay gratification. Another indication is your ability to take care of children's needs and understand why their needs so often must take priority.

How you feel when others' needs assume priority is part of your maturity. This is not to say, by any means, that you do not have a right to have your needs met or that you must always defer to others in needs priorities. Nothing could be further from the truth. However, if you are saddened, angered, etc., when others' needs seem to have priority over yours, you may want to reflect on whether you assume that your needs should always have priority. Do you feel more deserving, and somewhat envious or jealous? This may signal your need to have others put your needs before theirs, most, or all the time which is an indication of some underdevelopment in understanding of the needs of others.

Expecting to be *in charge* as a characteristic of entitlement is very similar to competitive behaviors that have power and control as their goal. The following list of behaviors can be reflective of competition to be in charge: expecting to give directions and orders, to be perceived as the leader or boss, and/or to empower others and have their ideas accepted over theirs. Ask yourself how often you engage in these behaviors at any level or intensity. Behaviors such as challenging, sulking, pushing others to agree, taking over and directing, sitting at the head of the table and talking over others are examples of behaviors that indirectly indicate a desire to be in charge. You may not be aware of the need or desire that underlies the behavior, and becoming more aware is the first step in addressing any assumption you may have that you should be in charge.

The destructive narcissist automatically assumes that he or she is so superior that of course he or she will be in charge. Destructive narcissist's basic needs are to regulate others, direct, overpower, be the center of attention, and to be perceived as superior. If for some reason they are not in charge, they will use the described competitive behaviors to undermine whomever is in charge.

Destructive narcissists will challenge by disagreeing or presenting another viewpoint with the intent of making the other person seem inept or stupid, push others to agree as an attempt to form a coalition against the leader or boss or to bolster their need for power and control, talk a lot to keep attention focused on them, and do or say things that suggest that they know more or can do better than the leader or boss.

This characteristic of entitlement can be seen in an attitude of disbelief that others do not always agree, the expectation that *others will always agree with them*, and anger or rage when there appears to be disagreement or opposition. There is a lack of openness to considering opinions, ideas, etc. from others and a marked lack of tolerance for opinions and ideas from others. These are automatically rejected as having no merit.

Adults may exhibit this attitude with children and adolescents, although adolescents are more likely to rebel. The attitude is that because he or she is the adult, children or adolescents cannot disagree. Some people feel that their spouse, or significant other, must always agree and become angry or disappointed when the spouse does not. This attitude may even be extended to the workplace, where colleagues and subordinates are expected always to agree and disagreement is not tolerated.

From whom do you expect automatic agreement to the extent that you become angry when the person does not agree with you? Reflect on the relationships or roles that these people have with you, such as that of a boss or spouse, and see if there is a pattern. There may be patterns of expecting agreement from others. For example, those considered to be less competent or inferior in some way, those who expect to show their love for you by always agreeing with you, and those who are extensions of you, such as your children.

Another reflection is on the level and intensity of emotions aroused in you when these people or a person does not agree. Is there a deep hurt that says that such people do not find you worthy and this is why they do not agree? Or is there a burning anger that seems to say "How dare you disagree, you must be seeking to destroy me?" Some variation of these two positions is indicative of an attitude of entitlement.

One entitlement attitude of the destructive narcissist that is very difficult for many to accept and deal with is an expectation that all *rewards and recognitions* are justified and should be given to him or her. It does not matter how little the destructive narcissist did—or even if it was nothing—the person should be recognized as the contributor and rewarded.

Elsewhere in the book there is a description of a person who talks with others, takes their ideas, and presents them as his or her own. This is one example of the entitlement attitude. This person probably believes that he or she has a right to be recognized for these ideas because, after all, the person presented them, although he or she did not develop them. This person does not have any awareness of the impact this behavior has on others and wonders why colleagues do not want to exchange ideas.

Children like having all the attention and want all the recognition and rewards. Gradually, they begin to understand how rewards, recognitions, and behaviors are connected and are able to tolerate having rewards and recognitions bestowed on others. Adults have usually learned that they must earn these and do not expect to be rewarded or recognized for making little or no contribution. Adults who have a destructive DNP, or some aspects that are similar to those of a DNP, can exhibit the entitlement attitude.

Another example is where rewards and recognitions are expected for everything someone does. This is an expectation that may be interpreted by others as low self-esteem, etc. However, some who meet this description have an entitlement attitude. The real motive is that they expect others to accept that they are more worthy than anyone else and to make sure they are given their due, that is, rewards and recognitions. This attitude can be seen in people who sulk or pout when you do not compliment them several times a day for any little thing they do. While it is usual for us to want our contributions recognized, most of us do not expect comments or compliments on everything, nor do we become profoundly disappointed or angry when our contributions go unrecognized. We save these intense reactions for those few times when we have objective evidence of our considerable contribution that is unrecognized and unrewarded.

One of the most irritating aspects of an entitlement attitude exhibited by a destructive narcissist is the one where there is the assumption that *rules and laws* are for everyone else. Individuals who have this attitude understand the rules and laws but see no need to conform to them, as the rules and laws prohibit them from attaining their goals and thus are of no value. However, they do insist that others obey the rules and laws.

This sense of entitlement is also related to wanting to be considered unique and special, so unique and special that it is understood by all that they are above or beyond being expected to conform to rules and laws. What may be confusing is that, except in extreme cases, most people with an entitlement attitude are not consistent in this expectation. That is, they conform to some rules and laws but not to others. What must be remembered is that when they do conform, they consider that they are entitled not to do so.

This attitude is similar to that of the antisocial personality but differs in motivation. An antisocial personality understands rules and laws, does not obey them, but acts this way out of a desire for revenge for neglect and abuse they may have suffered. The antisocial acts are a lashing out in an attempt to hurt others as the person himself or herself has been hurt. The entitlement attitude does not contain a revenge motive but is derived from an unconscious, ingrained assumption about being unique and special and an indifference or complete disregard for the rights of others.

An example of an attitude of being above or beyond rules and laws that is mild and somewhat common is speeding. Speed limits are clearly posted, but most people routinely disregard them. Posted speed limits appear to be only suggestions, and many become irate when stopped by a police officer and given a speeding ticket. The posted speed limits did not apply to them: the limits applied to others.

Destructive narcissists ride roughshod over any rule or law deemed to be in their way and have no idea of why others find this behavior offensive. In truth, they probably do not care that others find it offensive. The only rules and laws they recognize are those that, if ignored, will have severe consequences for them, such as going to jail. Indeed, many do not think they will ever be caught, and when they are, become indignant. For example, many white-collar criminals have this attitude.

CHAPTER 6

How You Contribute to Your Own Distress

You play a major role in the distressing effects you experience when interacting with people who have a destructive narcissistic pattern. Contributing to your distress are the following:

- The extent of your emotional susceptibility.
- Old parental messages that continue to exert major influences on your behavior, attitudes, feelings, and perceptions about your self, your needs, wishes, desires, and your fantasies.
- Lingering aspects of your underdeveloped narcissism.
- Poor boundary strength.

EMOTIONAL CONTAGION

Emotions can be caught from others, especially primitive emotions, such as anger and fear. Primitive emotional contagion is present from birth and is somewhat automatic, unintentional, and uncontrollable, as it exists on the nonconscious or unconscious level.

There is considerable research that demonstrates emotional contagion between parents and their children. Parents catch emotions from their children and children catch emotions from their parents. There is also evidence that parents and children can communicate emotions to and from each other beginning at birth. Emotions between the nurturer and infant or child are clues to the quality of the relationship, and the more responsive the nurturer is to emotional expressiveness and needs of the infant, the more likely there is to be healthy psychological development.

There is also considerable evidence from the literature on clinical research for emotional contagion for therapists, during therapy. The nature and quality of the therapeutic relationship depends in part on the therapist's ability to access the feelings of the client. These feelings can be caught by the therapist, who empathically understands what the client is feeling by the reactions generated in him or her, such as when the client feels anxious, fearful, depressed, or angry, and the therapist echoes these feelings.

Emotional contagion, especially primitive emotional contagion, provides a research basis for discussing how and why you can be emotionally susceptible without knowing that you are catching others' emotions and acting on them as if they were your own. These are actions and reactions that appear to be somewhat common in interactions with a destructive narcissist. Understanding what they are, how they may operate, and susceptibility to emotional contagion provides a foundation for suggesting strategies that can prevent experiencing many of the negative feelings, such as frustration and devaluation that are common in interactions with someone who has a DNP.

However, we are not going to tackle theories about how the self develops nor try to define what the self is, except to note that the self referred to in this discussion is concerned with the personhood of the individual. We are starting with the premise that the self is in existence for every individual.

It may be helpful to try to visualize your self as having two parts, the good self and the bad self. The good self has all the positive characteristics, such as worthwhile, strong, competent, responsible, lovable, and dependable, etc. The bad self has all the negative characteristics, such as ineptness, prone to failure, incompetent, inadequate, wrong, etc. Your good self has statements about you such as "I am capable," "I am lovable," "I am worthwhile and valued." Your bad self has statements such as "I am so bad," "I will never be able to do anything right," "I always fail," "I am very inadequate." The characteristics and self-statements develop from experiences with parents and others who nurture, care, and interact with you from birth and can continue all your life. The process of developing the self begins with birth, and some feel that the care and nurturing of the infant sets a pattern for development of the self that can be modified or changed only with great difficulty.

Projection, projective identification, and identification are some concepts that can help you understand what happens when you interact with someone who has a destructive narcissistic pattern, and why you can end up experiencing distressing feelings that linger. Projection, projective identification, and identification are processes used by the self; projection to try and get rid of "bad" or unacceptable parts of self, projective identification to get rid of the bad or unacceptable parts of self and to manipulate others, and identification to define parts of self. Projection and projective identification involve splitting off unacceptable parts of self, and projective identification and identification involve taking in from others and incorporating something into one's self, and acting on the incorporated part. Each concept is explained and illustrated. You can experience all three of these in interactions with someone who has a DNP.

PROJECTION

Projection begins when someone has an unacceptable thought or feeling, such as disgust. This feeling is unacceptable to this person because it is uncomfortable, fearful, or anxiety producing. That person does not wish to feel this way, and, on an unconscious level, tries to get rid of the feeling by putting it on someone else. Or, the person may be feeling disgusted with his or her behavior or self-perception, and because these feelings are unacceptable he or she gets rid of them by projecting them on someone else. It should be noted that projection is only one way of getting rid of these unacceptable feelings; there are other ways. For example, repression could also be used to get rid of these feelings. When repression is used, the feelings are not projected on someone else; they are pushed into the unconscious, and the person is no longer aware of them.

One other thing happens in projection. After the unacceptable feeling is projected on to the other person, the projector then reacts as if the receiver has the projected unacceptable feelings or characteristics. For example, if digust was projected, the reaction to the receiver would be as if he or she was disgusting or as if the person was disgusted with the projector, when in fact the receiver was neither disgusting nor felt disgust! It becomes easier to understand how some misperceptions and misunderstandings occur when projections are a part of communications. Further complicating matters is that all this projecting is taking place on an unconscious level.

Projection is an important concept when discussing the Destructive Narcissistic Pattern, as people with a DNP usually have powerful projections. They generally disown all unacceptable thoughts and feelings about self and project them on to others, such as, you, and then react to others (you) as if these others had the projected thought or feeling. When the destructive narcissist does this projection, you are often left with feeling that he or she feels you are incompetent or whatever trait was projected. You may even ask yourself frequently, "Why does he or she act (or feel) as if I cannot do anything right?" as a result of their projections.

Categories of Projections. Projections can be categorized in two ways, when discussing the DNP; disliked parts of self, and unmet or unresolved needs. These are not the only categories, but they are used here as illustrations.

What you dislike most in yourself is what you are most likely to project onto others. For example, if you do not like the idea that you make mistakes, then you will become irate at others for the least perceived mistake. If you are unaccepting of your anger, then you are unaccepting of anger in others. You could be the receiver of what the destructive narcissist finds unacceptable about him or herself.

Having unmet needs or unresolved needs for acceptance, affection, and power, etc., can also result in projections. People who are seeking to have these needs met may project on to others that they have these characteristics and then react to them as if they do have them and can therefore meet their needs, when in reality they may or may not have the characteristics.

The following list presents some statements that can be indicative of projections, and a possible projection related to the statement.

Statements	Possible Projection
No one appreciates me	I do not appreciate others or let them know I appreciate them
My spouse never listens to me	Many times I tune out my spouse
Everyone is dishonest	I am dishonest in some ways
You're wonderful	I am wonderful at times
People are always putting me down	I often depreciate others

AN EXERCISE IN PROJECTION

The following exercise can help you become more aware of some of your possible projections. You may want to try it for admiration, disliked traits, and unmet needs projections.

Divide a sheet of paper into half lengthwise so that you have two columns. Label one column with the name of someone you dislike or with whom you have a conflict. In that column list all characteristics of that person that irritate, annoy, or anger you. Label the second column "Me." List some criticisms others, not necessarily the person in column 1, have made of you. You do not have to accept or agree with the criticism in order to list it.

Now compare the two lists for similarities, not necessarily in the same degree or to the same extent, but for similar characteristics, behaviors, or attitudes. The similarities are indicative of possible projections.

Review both columns and become aware of what possible projections may exist.

PROJECTIVE IDENTIFICATION

Even more complex than the concept of projection is the concept of projective identification. Projective identification occurs when unacceptable or disowned parts of the self are projected onto another person and that person accepts the projection (an introjection), and incorporates the projection, identifies with it, and reacts or acts accordingly. Some even suggest that the projector causes the other person to react or act in accord with the projection. In projection, the receiver does not accept the projection, as is the case for projective identification.

The next piece in projective identification is the projector maintaining contact with the projection. The projector gets rid of it but continues to stay in touch with it in the other person. Maintaining contact promotes the next step, which is attempting to control the recipient through the projection. The final step is an unconscious induction in the recipient of that which was projected. An example of the process is that the projector feels angry and the anger is intolerable, so it is projected onto the recipient, who is then manipulated by the projected anger to the point where anger is induced in him or her.

An example may help to clarify this process. Have you ever had an argument with someone, realized that you were becoming very angry, and wondered why you were so angry? You started out relatively okay, may be a little irritated or annoyed, but the more you interacted with the person, the more this feeling intensified and you couldn't seem to control it. You may even have done or said things you did not mean, but could not stop. What may have happened is the following, and all occurred on the unconscious level.

- The other person in the argument was angry, but did not accept the anger.
- The person got rid of his or her anger by projecting it on you.
- You accepted the projected anger (introjection) that then intensified your original annoyance.
- The other person stayed in touch with his or her projected anger (which is now a part of your original annoyance), and manipulated it to get you to act on it and you did.
- Once the other person got you to act, he or she lets go of the projection, and you were left with the intense feeling of anger. The other person was OK, but you were fuming.

Reflect on a past experience with someone you have identified as having a DNP, and determine if you possibly experienced a projective identification.

USES OF PROJECTIVE IDENTIFICATION

There are five ways that projective identification can be used: as a defense mechanism, as a way to communicate, as a desire or need to share feelings, as a mechanism to learn new ways, and to scapegoat someone. Use as a defense mechanism occurs to protect against experiencing intolerable feelings. The projector can disown that which is projected, but it remains viable in the recipient. Used as a way to communicate, projective identification attempts to force the recipient to experience feelings similar to those of the projector. The desire or need to share feelings assumes that the recipient is not entirely unique and different and that he or she must share the feelings of the projector. The most constructive use of a projective identification is to identify with and learn from the recipient ways of coping with projections. Scapegoating someone means that the projector attacks that which was projected into the recipient and also induced in him or her. It was intolerable in the projector, and is also perceived by the projector as unacceptable in the recipient.

PROJECTIVE IDENTIFICATION AND THE DNP

Projective identification is also a very important concept to consider when discussing the Destructive Narcissistic Pattern because it helps explain some of the feelings, frustration, and confusion you experience after interacting with someone who has a DNP. Many people walk away from an interaction with a destructive narcissist feeling churned up, angry, anxious, inadequate, incompetent, attacked, disconnected, and devalued, and wondering what happened to produce such intense, uncomfortable emotions. In addition, they are generally frustrated and confused. For those of us who do a lot of introspection, we generally start asking ourselves what unresolved issues we have that are producing these feelings. Even this self-examination does not produce satisfactory answers, although we do recognize how our unresolved issues have been triggered. The following scenario is an example.

You go in to ask your supervisor about getting a new computer. At that point, if you were asked how you felt, you would respond, "Fine." In previous conversations, the computer you have was acknowledged by the supervisor to be out-of-date and lacking sufficient capacity to get the job done. As you make your inquiry, you are confronted with a barrage of questions asking you to name each piece of work you could not do in the past year because of the inadequate computer, why you did not do the work, and what your justification is for a new computer. Along the way, devaluing comments are made about the quality of your work. You find yourself getting more and more frustrated, angry, and confused, and may even ask yourself whether you remember correctly the supervisor agreeing in the past that the computer was inadequate. You may also feel discounted, incompetent, and somehow "wrong." The discussion concludes with the supervisor saying that he or she will explore the feasibility of getting you a new computer but that the supervisor is not sure one is justified. You leave all churned up, questioning yourself about what happened. Yes, you may be angry at the supervisor, but you do not understand why you are as angry as you are and why you are also experiencing all these other feelings. Although you usually get over or moderate your reaction to dissent or discord fairly quickly and easily, your reactions to this interaction remain with you for a much longer time. You may even develop a headache or stomach upset.

Projective identification can explain much of what happened. The destructive narcissist got rid of the unacceptable feelings, such as anger, frustration, confusion, and feeling discounted and/or inadequate, by projecting them onto you. You incorporated and identified with them and acted accordingly. Whereas you did not have these feelings before the interaction, you took them in as projected, and now you are experiencing them, causing you to wonder, "What happened?" Interestingly, the destructive narcissist usually feels great after these interactions, and everyone else feels lousy.

All this takes place on an unconscious level. The person with a DNP is not aware that he or she is projecting, nor are you aware that you have incorporated, identified, and acted on the projections. This person has gotten rid of the unacceptable part of self, caused you to act on it, and now can feel justified in rejecting or devaluing you because you have exhibited those reprehensible characteristics and behaviors.

POWERFUL SENDERS

Those who have the ability to infect others with their emotions seem to have the following characteristics: they are able to feel strong emotions or appear to do so; they can express strong emotions through their facial, vocal, or postural activity; and they are relatively insensitive, indifferent, and unresponsive when others are experiencing emotions different from theirs. Although both positive and negative emotions can be sent and caught, negative emotions, such as sadness and anxiety, are more likely to be sent and caught. Destructive narcissists are very powerful senders and can prevent their catching others' feelings.

Some emotionally susceptible people are more open to emotional contagion and share many of the following characteristics.

- They are very aware of others' emotions and attend to these rather than ignore them.
- They perceive themselves as interrelated with others rather than completely independent of others.
- They are adept at reading emotional nonverbal communication such as voices and gestures.
- They tend to assume the bodily positions and facial expressions of others when talking with them.
- They can be very emotionally self-aware.
- They are emotionally reactive.

This description underscores the susceptibility of therapists, teachers, and other caretakers to emotional contagion, as their personality and professional expectations meet many of the characteristics for emotional susceptibility, and it is important that they experience their own emotions and not "catch" those of others.

However, there are those who are resistant to emotional contagion: people who have power over others, people who dislike or hate the person communicating, and those who are focused primarily on their own interests. Those with a DNP certainly can meet one or more of these criteria. They are powerful projectors but are less prone to catching others' emotions.

IDENTIFICATION

One set of responses to the destructive narcissist is identification. Identification, on a nonconscious or unconscious level, is a defense to protect against the perceived threat of destruction of the self. It can be triggered by projective identifications of that person, but can also rise from within the individual because of his or her own underdeveloped narcissism.

Identification with the destructive narcissist refers to the action of assuming the troubling traits or characteristics displayed by that person. The terrifying part, for me, about the response is that you are not aware that you are doing this, that is, identifying, and if you are not also aware of the threat or possibility that you can or may identify, you do not even take a critical look at yourself to monitor your behavior. The traits or characteristics with which you identify could provide you with considerable information about the parts of self not seen by you if, or when, awareness emerges, or is considered as a possibility and is explored and examined.

There must be something in the receiver that allows him or her to receive the projection, and identify with it. That something may be a similarity or a difference. In addition, the receiver may have inadequate boundary strength, and this inadequacy can be either in general or in a specific area. Most often this occurs on an unconscious level not under your control. The extent to which your boundaries are fluid, weak, unstable, or ill-defined contributes to the conscious and unconscious willingness to accept a projection. The strength and stability of your boundaries contribute to your ability to block or insulate against projections, both on the conscious and unconscious levels.

Blocking projections, or insulating your self against projections may be very difficult especially when there is a close relationship between the receiver and the sender. There are numerous similarities between the two, and this can permit the projections to gain access to the recipient almost anywhere. This is one of the reasons why mothers can find it difficult to block projections from their children, lovers from each other, and victims from emotional abusers.

When there are inadequate but well-developed boundaries it is easier to block or insulate against projections, as the sender can only gain access at particular points. Defenses, such as blocking, need only be employed in that direction. This is one of the reasons why some people find the projective identifications of the destructive narcissist more tolerable than do others. Another part of toleration is the extent to which the projection triggers identification in the recipient.

Similarities and complementaries in specific areas are two conditions that promote acceptance of projective identifications. This means that there are aspects of the projector and recipient that are held in common or are complementary, that is, different in ways that enhance each other. Similarities such as gender, race, class, and role allow both to make greater efforts to understand and feel each other, thereby promoting an acceptance of projective identifications. Complementarity in specific areas also promotes acceptance because of the conscious realization of the contributions of the other, thereby promoting those conditions that favor acceptance of projective identifications.

Inadequate psychological boundaries, similarities, and complementaries do not fully explain the reason there is acceptance of projective identifications. However, these do provide a beginning for exploration of why the powerful projections and projective identifications found in those who have a DNP affect us the way they do, and they also provide suggestions for strategies to help block or insulate against experiencing them. Understanding where our ego boundaries are inadequate, and whether they are weak and unstable, or strong and stable allows us to mount defenses in needed places while we work to build or strengthen ego boundaries.

Another area for exploration is the extent to which we and the destructive narcissist are similar or complement each other. This is also somewhat difficult to do as we resist accepting that we have some traits in common with that person; that we have not sufficiently developed appropriate narcissism in some areas; or that the destructive narcissist has complementarity with us in one or more specific areas. However, this self-exploration and introspection can be very fruitful in developing adequate defenses against the projective identifications found in those who have a DNP. The following example illustrates this recommended process for self-examination, and recognition of the possible projections, projective identifications, and identifications that could be present.

ANALYSES OF INTERACTIONS WITH A DNP

After dealing with someone who was likely a destructive narcissist over several months, I developed a list of characteristics and behaviors associated with the person. I then reflected on my behaviors and/or changes during the same time frame and noted which of my behaviors were similar to that person's, which began during the time period, and those that increased in number and/or intensity. I assumed that we both had some behaviors and attitudes in common. I may have controlled some of mine, but they were not unique to me.

The next step was to examine my perceptions of changes in colleagues' behavior, those who also had interactions with the destructive narcissist. I focused on changes or examples of previously unseen behaviors. There were numerous similarities.

The final step was to solicit some colleagues' input as to their perceptions of changes in their own behavior and that of other colleagues, especially behaviors that negatively impacted relationships. The following lists were generated. The first list presents behaviors of the destructive narcissist. The second list describes feelings and behaviors exhibited by me and others that were not characteristic of us, or that had increased in number or intensity. Note: As a group my colleagues and I displayed all the feelings and behaviors in List 2, although no one person displayed all of the feelings and behaviors in this list. The person with a DNP did display all the behaviors in the list.

List 1—Observed Behaviors of the Person with a DNP
- Criticizes constantly.
- Is angry at perceived slights, blaming, and so forth.
- Gives orders and expects them to be obeyed promptly.
- Complains constantly about not feeling appreciated.
- Nags.
- Verbally abuses others.
- Devalues others and their work or accomplishments.
- Lacks empathy.
- Is unable to be pleased by anyone or anything.
- Takes over space, resources.
- Second-guesses others' work.
- Blames and finds fault.

List 2—Behaviors and Feelings Exhibited and Experienced by Others
- A lessening or withdrawal of empathy for fellow colleagues.
- Feels unappreciated.
- Feels that work, efforts, and productivity are unrecognized.

- Feels excluded.
- Second-guesses others' work.
- Verbally abuses others.
- Is hypersensitive to perceived criticism, slights, and so forth.
- Openly displays anger, usually inappropriately.
- Makes disparaging and/or devaluing remarks about others.

OUTCOMES FOR UNIT IN EXAMPLE

After reviewing and confirming identifications, a somewhat objective analysis was made on the impact and outcomes that occurred from receiving the destructive narcissist's projections and identifying with some or all of them. Among the most obvious impacts and outcomes were reduced creativity; more constriction and less spontaneity; increased alertness to conspiracies and intrigue; increased backbiting and nit-picking; increased empathic failures; inability to overlook minor irritations and annoyances; increased documenting of activities, requests and the like; more outbursts of anger; a withdrawal from or pulling in of contact with others; and increased competitive behavior together with a decrease in cooperative or collaborative behavior. In short, the entire unit began to display the characteristics of the DNP, and members introjected and reported many of the same feelings that are characteristic of the DNP, such as emptiness.

DISCUSSION

Identification with some of the behaviors, attitudes, and feelings of a DNP speaks of the destructiveness of attempting to have any kind of relationship with this person where individuals are unaware of what is occurring. The unconscious projective identifications and subsequent introjective identifications combine to be corrosive and erode productivity as well as any relationships. The actions of individuals in the unit described previously reveal an unconscious or nonconscious collaboration with the destructive narcissist to maintain the ego defenses. The people in the unit became empty, suspicious, unable or unwilling to empathize, and much less creative. The healthy adult narcissistic characteristics proposed by Kohut (1997), creativity, empathy, and humor, were muted. Even relatively healthy narcissism in adults can be adversely affected, leading to considerable self-doubt and eroding of self-confidence.

MODERATING THE IMPACT

This part of the discussion focuses on moderating the impact of identification with behaviors, attitudes, and feelings of someone with a DNP. This presentation looks at one's internal resources through introspection, personal associations with the introjected projections from the destructive narcissist, old parental messages, and cognitive distortions as ways of understanding the impact of the destructive narcissist on oneself and developing responses in accord with one's own needs. We begin and emphasize self-understanding, not on the person with a DNP. This emphasis empowers you to better defend yourself, withstand the negative feelings and impact that can emerge in interactions with a destructive narcissist, and can show you where your underdeveloped narcissism is helping to contribute to your distress.

INTROSPECTION

Introspection is the first step. Taking a look at personal behaviors and attitudes or feelings to identify those that are not usual, have increased or decreased, or are troubling to you or to others with whom you have important relationships, and looking at the reemergence of old issues are all part of introspection. Realizing that you are dissatisfied with your responses to the person, but not blaming yourself can begin the process.

A word about blaming yourself. Many people, especially those who can empathize with others, are prone to feel they are at fault or have in some way failed to be all that they perceived themselves to be. The cycle of dissatisfaction with self—increased efforts to understand the destructive narcissist and/or to empathize, and the resulting failure to alter the situation, can lead to increased feelings of inadequacy, frustration, etc., and dissatisfaction with self—results in acceleration of withdrawal and despair. It seems that the more effort one puts into the relationship, the more frustration and self-doubt increase. If you have the perception of self that you are responsible for the frustration because of your unresolved issues or incomplete psychological development, you blame yourself.

Perhaps the first step in introspection is to accept that you have limitations and that you are not to blame. This is not to say that the other person is to blame, but to acknowledge that you are contributing to your own distress if you blame yourself. This may be somewhat difficult to do as those people who accept responsibility for their feelings also may accept the idea that they choose to be frustrated, angry, and so forth, and the other person cannot or does not "make" them have these feelings. Basically, this is true. However, if one is not aware of projections and possible projective identifications, both of which are unconscious processes, then one is not aware that what is experienced is both under one's control and not under one's control.

Once you can accept the fact that not only are you not to blame but that you may or do have personal issues that impact and influence your responses, you can begin to explore the extent to which these personal issues contribute to your personal reactions to the destructive narcissist and develop strategies for dealing with your reactions.

ASSOCIATIONS

The next step is to identify the associations that connect the introjected identifications. For example, if you identify with the characteristic lack of empathy and become less empathic, what associations can you make with previous experiences? Was there a time when you were not empathic because of hurt or fear? Is being empathic associated with feelings of betrayal? Do you know from exploration of personal issues that you had a significant reverse parental experience in childhood, where you were made to feel responsible for a parent or parent's feelings, and not empathizing became your way of not being overwhelmed by the emotions of others? These questions and others can illuminate the associations. Once these are identified, you can begin to understand your reactions and subsequent behaviors with respect to the destructive narcissist and with others, for it would be unlikely that others also feel a lessening of your empathy in interactions with them.

One process for identifying your associations is free association. This can be done with a tape recorder to record your responses or by writing responses. Begin with a feeling, situation, event, or image that involves the destructive narcissist with the intent of opening yourself to true responding without reflection or editing. Whatever comes to mind will be spoken or written.

Keeping the feeling, situation, event, or image in mind, write or record everything that emerges as a thought or feeling. Words, phrases, fragments, and so forth, must all be noted. Write or record until the flow of responses ceases or you find yourself thinking in order to come up with a response.

Once the list has been generated, reread or listen to it. As you read or listen, what other connections emerge? How are the responses, or parts of responses, linked or further associated? The links or associations will usually be from previous relationships and/or time periods. At this point, some understandings will occur. It may be helpful to record or write the understandings and continue to explore more associations. The next session focuses on understanding your associations.

OLD PARENTAL MESSAGES

Some associations may be parental messages that speak of your flaws or inadequacies. That is, the destructive narcissist's verbalizations or actions may trigger remembered parental injunctions, feelings, evaluations, etc. that continue to impact the you and influence your functioning and relationships, albeit on an unconscious level. Everyone still has some of these old parental messages even if they are not aware of them and how they continue to exert influences.

These are verbal and nonverbal messages sent by parents to children and received, either clearly or with distortions, and introjected. These messages that define how others react to them are one way children begin to develop self-esteem. Mirroring of the child's perception of himself or herself by parents is one facet of building healthy narcissism. The parent who approves of and delights in the child is mirroring the child's perception of self, that is, "I am lovable," and conveys this through word and deed.

This is also the process by which the child learns what is acceptable and what is not. Embedded in the learning may be the message that the child is flawed, not just the behavior but the essential self, and this is shameful to both the parent and the child. There are many such messages sent by parents verbally and nonverbally, consciously and unconsciously.

One way of knowing if old parental messages are being triggered and reacted to is listening to your feelings when interacting or after interacting with the DNP. If you feel much as you did when you were a child, there are probably old parental messages being reactivated. If you feel patronized, talked down to, impotent, furious and/or fatally flawed, then there are parental messages being received. This is not to suggest that the destructive narcissist is not doing or saying patronizing things, or blaming, and so forth, but it is your reaction to what they are doing or saying that is indicative of old parental messages and unresolved issues around them. Becoming aware of and continuing to work on these issues can do much to moderate the impact of this person on you.

COGNITIVE DISTORTIONS

Another approach is to look at possible cognitive distortions you may have about yourself and/or others to determine whether they can be modified, leading to less emotional distress. Examples of cognitive distortions include extremism, focusing on the negative, "awfulizing," all-or-nothing thinking, overpersonalization, and "shouldism." Each will be briefly described.

Extremism. Extremism occurs when thinking patterns try to categorize almost everything into polarities, such as good and bad. There is no room or consideration for shades of gray; whatever, it is either black or white. This kind of cognitive distortion makes for very rigid thought and evaluation of self and others. When the destructive narcissist criticizes or blames, extremism causes the person's response to be either he or she is right and I am very wrong, or he or she is wrong and I am right. In either case, communication ceases and emotional distress can occur from resentment or anger at being right but not perceived as such by that person, or shame and humiliation experienced for being wrong.

Focusing on the negative. Another cognitive distortion occurs when you focus only on the negative and overlook or ignore any positive aspects. This is not to suggest that everything is always positive; everything has a negative side, and this should not be discounted. However, a constant focus only on the negative leads to self-fulfilling prophecy—things are bad or miserable.

Anxiety and misery is increased when the cognitive distortion of focusing on the negative is employed during or after interactions with the destructive narcissist. A tendency to select the negative and emphasize or even obsess over it can accelerate a depressive spiral. Those with a DNP are blaming and critical of others and say or do things to make others feel inadequate, incompetent, and fatally flawed. If the receiver has the cognitive distortion of focusing on the negative, this attitude helps the destructive narcissist by the receiver not only agreeing with the destructive narcissist's evaluation, but also adding to it with additional negative thoughts about the self.

"Awfulizing." Awfulizing is similar to focusing on the negative but takes it considerably further. This cognitive distortion assumes that doom or dire consequences lie around the corner almost always and should be foremost in one's thoughts. The person does not know what to do and becomes paralyzed at the awful possibilities that "may occur." He or she fears to do anything, fears doing nothing, and thus is left paralyzed, with a strong sense of dread and doom.

People who awfulize are paralyzed in the sense of taking action. They may be somewhat hysterical otherwise, with lots of talk about the awfulness and the impending dire consequences. They flail around trying to decide what to do and dump on anyone who will listen to their sense of awfulness and impending doom. A destructive narcissist is very good at expanding and intensifying this cognitive distortion by pushing the person to "do something," with the added caveat that whatever he or she does will be wrong and the destructive narcissist knows this and will also be there to point out how wrong it was and how inadequate the person is.

All-or-nothing thinking. All-or-nothing cognitive distortions describe an individual who speaks and thinks in terms such as always and never. For example, if someone does something in error, the person's thought or response would be that this person is always wrong—not that he or she made an error this time. This cognitive distortion does not allow for a holistic appraisal of self and of others; it focuses on one specific thing and generalizes to the whole from that one thing.

This cognitive distortion also demands that the self and others be perfect; there is no in between, no allowance made for mistakes, no recognition of limitations. The self and others are perceived as flawed or inadequate unless they are perfect. For example, someone who uses this cognitive distortion would not be pleased with birthday gifts unless each and every one was exactly what he or she wanted. The person would reflect, maybe even obsess, on the part that was not perfect, ignoring all the gifts that were what was wanted. He or she may even say, "I never get what I want," or something similar.

Overpersonalization. Overpersonalization occurs when an individual personalizes everything and reacts accordingly. No matter what is being said or done, this person reacts as though it were a personal slight, put down, or criticism. People who overpersonalize act as though someone is blaming them or expecting them to assume responsibility, and they become angry. This cognitive distortion may arise from old parental messages or other experiences when growing up, such as, having the responsibility to see that others' needs are taken care of and receiving the message that you are "bad" if you do not do a good job. An example of overpersonalization is when you feel you have failed or ought to take action if someone mentions being uncomfortable, unless of course, you are responsible for their comfort, such as when you are a host or a hostess.

People who overpersonalize will find it very uncomfortable to interact with the destructive narcissist because this person's projections will tap into their feelings and assumptions that the destructive narcissist's feelings are their responsibility and they are not doing an adequate job of taking care of this person. The strong parental messages are reactivated, producing profound feelings of inadequacy, incompetence, and self-doubt. This cognitive distortion allows people to beat themselves up more than the person with a DNP does.

"Shouldism." "Shoulds" and "oughts" can be both good and bad. Cultural expectations and values are transmitted and incorporated by the individual to provide directions for acceptable behaviors, and used in that way, they

tell the person what is "good" and what is "bad." For example, in most U.S. communities people are taught that one should be polite, and polite behaviors are modeled and taught. The definition of polite may differ from community to community, but everyone in a particular community knows what he or she should do.

However, shoulds and oughts become cognitive distortions when an individual does not actively select a particular course of action, but only does what he or she feels should or ought to be done, acts contrary to his or her self-interest all the time, and subjugates his or her needs so that others are taken care of constantly. The person with a DNP triggers and intensifies this cognitive distortion, and the individual is miserable because he or she should be able to do whatever is needed, such as take care of the destructive narcissist. This cognitive distortion readily plays into the grandiose and entitlement assumptions of the person with a DNP that others should and must meet their spoken and unspoken needs.

This chapter presented several concepts and ways that illustrate how you may help contribute to your own distress. Since you cannot change people with a destructive narcissistic pattern, and they are unlikely to think that they need to change, your best recourse for helping yourself is to understand why you are affected as you are, to fortify and build your boundaries, and to reduce your underdeveloped narcissism.

CHAPTER 7
Intense Feelings: Anger, Fear, Guilt, and Shame

This chapter begins with descriptions for intense and uncomfortable feelings produced by interactions with destructive narcissists. Some of these feelings are also experienced by them, or they work hard and employ defenses to keep from experiencing them. Also discussed is narcissistic wounding that seems to trigger narcissistic rage. We begin with the narcissistic wounding and rage, discuss how anger, fear, guilt, and shame are usual reactions to a destructive narcissist but are not helpful for you, and provide suggestions for coping with these intense feelings.

NARCISSISTIC WOUNDING

Narcissistic wounding occurs when there is a deep hurt to the essential self and the receiver feels in danger of being abandoned and/or destroyed, inadequate, and/or defective. These feelings in turn can lead to other feelings such as shame for being flawed, and guilt for not being good enough. Although the words or action(s) triggered the wounding, much of what is experienced as wounding arises from within that person. Examples for reactions experienced from, or as narcissistic wounding, include the following:

- You try hard to not react and to forgive, but cannot let go of the negative feelings triggered by the words or actions of that person.
- You try to convince yourself that the person was not trying to hurt you, but some part of you does not accept that.

- You become hurt or enraged when you perceive someone, intentionally or unintentionally, as critical of you, blames you, or devalues you in some way.
- You continually wonder why you cannot be acceptable to others as you are, and why they think it necessary that you change.
- You frequently experience feelings of inadequacy, guilt, and/or shame.
- You carry considerable resentment over a long period of time.

Narcissistic wounding can begin early in life, and some of these early deep wounds do not heal, they become a part of the person and can be easily reinjured. This is one of the reasons why seemingly trivial remarks or actions can produce considerable hurt, and other such responses. You may even recognize that you are overreacting, but are helpless to prevent it.

These are wounds that may never completely heal, but can heal to a point where they are tolerable and don't cause you to get reinjured easily, or to overreact. Learning to access, contain, and manage your feelings is a large part of the growing and healing process.

Almost everyone, has experienced narcissistic injury, and many people have experienced this numerous times. Following are a few examples of situations that can produce narcissistic wounding.

- Rejection
- Breakup of a relationship
- Betrayal
- Unfair accusations
- Abandonment, even when uncontrollable or unintended
- Death
- Loss of anything or anyone where there is an emotional attachment
- Being shamed by someone such as a parent, a teacher, or a minister
- Prejudice and intolerance
- Being teased about something or someone you cannot change, or over which you have no control, such as body shape, poverty, or intelligence

The list of such situations can be very long. The extent and intensity of your reaction to these wounding events is dependent on the depth and kind of early narcissistic wounding you experienced. That is, if you had early wounding that has not healed, subsequent events will produce re-injury to that wound thereby increasing and intensifying your hurt and response.

Some of the early wounding may have taken place in the pre-verbal stage before you developed the cognitive skills that enable you to retreive memories in words or images that can ge expressed, so that understanding your earliest wounds becomes more difficult and impossible. What you can work on that will be healing, is to understand when you are narcissistically hurt, and to use some self-talk to soothe the hurt. There are some coping strategies presented in later chapters. This chapter focuses on understanding why you respond or feel as you do in situations with people who have a DNP, and why some strategies will not work.

NARCISSISTIC RAGE

The person with a DNP resists becoming narcissistically wounded, and when he or she senses the possibility, their narcissistic rage is triggered. Another term that needs definition for this discussion is "narcissistic rage", which can be a reaction to feelings of helplessness because of the inability to control others. Narcissistic rage is a response when the self feels threatened. This threat may be fantasized, that is, it is not real, but the person's self feels in danger and mounts the rage defense for protection and to destroy the threat. Narcissistic rage is expressed in many ways, such as devaluing of others, verbal attacks, contempt, argumentativeness, jealousy, sulking, and so on. The self is felt to be under attack and must be defended against being destroyed or abandoned. For example, if you can become aware of being irritated and admit to yourself that you are irritated, then begin to examine what you are reacting to and how it was wounding to your self narcissistically; it then becomes possible to decide to let it go or work through it rather than allowing irritations to build up so that it increases to annoyance or anger.

Imagine a baby who is frustrated, upset at not getting his or her needs met, lacking the language ability to communicate these needs, and does not have any understanding or interest in why his or her needs are not met promptly or adequately. You, as the caretaker, are trying to understand what the baby wants or needs, have tried several things all to no avail, understand that reasoning cannot be used because the infant's language and thinking skills are not developed, and you are frustrated, upset, and may even feel somewhat inadequate.

Now that you have visualized that situation, shift it as an overlay to an interaction you may have had with a destructive narcissist where you encountered the same feelings as did the caretaker in the described situation. Because this person is an adult, you may have tried logic and reasoning, or understanding and empathy. (It might have been a mistake to try empathy.) But, nothing is working. What you do not realize or accept, is that you are dealing with a very ticked off baby who cannot adequately communicate his or her needs, is experiencing narcissistic wounding as a consequence, and is in the throes of narcissistic rage. Nothing you say or do makes a dent in his or her rage.

Narcissistic rage is used as a defense against fears of abandonment and/or destruction, and these can be very intense for the destructive narcissist. Anger, in its most intense forms, is one of the two emotions that people with a DNP tend to experience intensely and deeply, with fear being the other emotion. Much of what they say to others, how they inflate their accomplishments, and so on; their indifference to others and other troubling behaviors and attitudes are designed to prevent them from experiencing anger and/or fear, and if they should emerge, the destructive narcissist quickly gets rid of them through projection on or into someone, or by repression and denial.

Everyone can experience narcissistic rage at some time, and it can be instructive to reflect on your experiences that could be narcissistic rage. Complicating the understanding are the indirect ways in which narcissistic rage is experienced and expressed. Indirect ways of experiencing and expressing narcissistic rage can be categorized as internal or external. Internal ways are when narcissistic rage is disguised and turned in on self or expressed to others in ambiguous or passive ways. It is important to the person who uses indirect expressions that the narcissistic rage must not be perceived as such by others because, if the rage is seen by others it will enable them to see the person's inadequacies and feelings of worthlessness. Examples of some internal ways of expressing narcissistic rage that reflect turning in on self are physical ailments, resentment, superrationality, suspiciousness, intellectualizing, teasing, sarcasm, forgetting, ignoring, and displacement.

External ways of expressing disguised narcissistic rage are those designed to make others feel uncomfortable or guilty and show them that they can be controlled. Examples of external expressions are acting helpless, demanding attention, deliberately frustrating others, sulking, pouting, devaluing others, blaming, criticizing, manipulating others, power plays, and sudden bursts of anger expression. Disguised narcissistic rage, however it is experienced and expressed, is a defense against knowing, or having others know, the degree to which you feel limited, inadequate, and fearful of being destroyed and/or abandoned.

Understanding some aspects of narcissistic rage allows for a deeper understanding of some of the behaviors of the destructive narcissist. Much of the internal and external experiencing for this person is to prevent self-awareness and others' awareness of their hungry, enraged, empty self: full of impotent anger, and fearful of a world that seems to reflect the hateful, worthless, vengeful, and contemptuous self. This inner experiencing is also part or most of what is projected on or into others and, if not understood to be a projection, causes considerable distress to the person who is the target of the projection.

Awareness is the first step in beginning to understand personal narcissistic rage. Accepting the degree to which our narcissistic rage experience and expression are internal or external provides guidelines for effecting change. This can be both personal growth and improvement of interpersonal relationships. The primary benefit, however, is that it will allow you to better block identification with narcissistic rage projected by the DNP.

COPING WITH THE DESTRUCTIVE NARCISSIST'S RAGE

Strategies for coping with the destructive narcissist's rage begin with understanding your own narcissistic rage. From your personal understanding comes a better understanding and tolerance for narcissistic rage expressed by others, even that in the DNP. This understanding provides you with armor when this person blames, criticizes, is contemptuous, lies, and so on. Your narcissistic rage is not as easily triggered by his or her actions and projections.

Other strategies include refusal to engage and to identify with the devaluing statements, an indifference to the consequences of the person's rage, and withdrawal. The primary point to remember is that you cannot change the destructive narcissist.

Refusal to engage means that you do not take exception, attack, or become defensive. You do not necessarily ignore what has been said, but it is a conscious decision not to take the interaction or discussions any further. You can moderate your tone of voice and make it calm, choose your words carefully, do not look them in the eye, slightly turn your body away, and start to change the subject. If they insist on continuing the discussion, listen and make only noncommittal comments that let them know you are listening. Don't forget that you are dealing with a ticked off baby.

Refusal to identify is more difficult to accomplish, as the devaluing, blaming, or criticizing statements can trigger your own insecurities. This is an instance where silently thinking of your self-affirming statements, such as saying to yourself that you have certain positive qualities, can be helpful. It keeps the focus off the downward spiral of negative perceptions.

Even more difficult to do is to *become indifferent* to the destructive narcissist's narcissistic rage. However, if you manage to do so, then your narcissistic rage will not be triggered by the remarks designed to wound, and you will not have interactions with that person that leave you feeling frustrating, angry, or hurt. Building a wall of indifference provides emotional insulation against projective identifications.

Withdrawal is just what it sounds like, you leave the room, the person, or the situation. This can be a physical withdrawal, or an emotional presence withdrawal. You have decided that you will not be a part of the interaction any longer.

Dealing with a destructive narcissist can arouse some intense and uncomfortable feelings for you. It may help to describe these so that you understand what you are feeling, and what the destructive narcissist may be feeling.

ANGER

Anger is a term used to describe an emotion that is experienced around perceptions of being threatened, thwarted, or frustrated, but is less intense than is narcissistic rage. However, one of the problems with any understanding or discussion of anger is the comprehensive way it is used to describe a feeling, with meanings ranging from irritation to fury. What one person may mean by the term is annoyance, while another person may understand what is being described as rage. It may be helpful to begin this discussion around anger as a response to interactions with a destructive narcissist and some definitions and descriptions of angry feelings.

It is important to make some distinctions about degrees of anger, both in order to understand personal reactions, as many times what is felt after interactions with a destructive narcissist is more intense than one's usual anger, and to understand the rage or fury that can be projected by the destructive narcissist. These distinctions also provide a structure for developing strategies for managing personal anger. The term "anger" will be used in this discussion as the level of expression midway between irritation and fury, that is, more intense than annoyance but much less intense than rage. Following is a continuum for anger ranging from mild irritation to extreme fury. Table 7.1 presents other feelings that the emotion may be defending against or that the person is experiencing, and a description of how it is experienced, and its outcome(s).

Table 7.1
Levels of Anger, Accompanying Feelings, and Potential Outcomes

Levels	Feelings	Outcomes
Irritation	Troubled, uncomfortable, miffed, and disturbed	Transitory, controlled
Annoyance	Frustration, impatience, prolonged discomfort provoked	A buildup of irksome events, suppressed or controlled
Anger	Threatened, excitement, displeasure, and vexation	Preparation for fight or flight, and racing thoughts
Rage	Wounded, betrayed, and rejected	Intense, unpredictable
Fury	Impotent, shame, abandonment, and destruction	Destructive, explosive, and irrational

MANAGING ANGRY FEELINGS

COGNITIVE DEFLECTION

Cognitive deflection refers to thinking about a reaction in addition to experiencing it. Infusing thoughts keeps a more balanced focus and can help keep feelings from increasing in intensity. This strategy is particularly useful when the response is anger, rage, or fury, although it is extremely difficult to use when furious. It can also be helpful when experiencing a projective identification by helping to identify which part of the reaction is your personal emotion and which part is the projection.

Cognitive deflection is a process where, cognitively or mentally, you are able to partially detach from the emotion and think about what is transpiring. You may already be aware of doing this sometimes, and can now begin to consciously do so. It may take some practice, but making the decision to use this category can allow you to more effectively understand and manage your narcissistic rage.

STRENGTHENING SELF-ESTEEM

Strengthening self-esteem and self-acceptance can be helpful in dealing with your own narcissistic rage, and also in reducing identification with others' projected rage, and the intensity of your emotions when triggered in interactions with a destructive narcissist.

Self-esteem can be dependent on the composition of the inner image to which you assess yourself, and on your capacity and ability to live up to that image. This use of the term points out the critical nature of the internal image together with your evaluation of self-efficacy needed to attain the level of that ideal image of your self. It also implies a realistic acceptance of limitations. How positively you regard and accept yourself as having both strengths and weaknesses plays an important role in helping to cope with personal narcissistic rage, and that of others.

Strengthening self-esteem can begin with a realistic appraisal of self, that is, one's assets and liabilities. Realistic means not indulging in false modesty nor glossing over limitations. Exercises to help you get started include making a list of assets, such as things you do well; strengths bombardment; and making a collage or drawing a picture of your greatest accomplishments. You may also want to take a look at those characteristics or behaviors that you consider to be liabilities. One way of becoming somewhat more objective about them is to identify a strength that could be embedded in the liability. For example, you may consider procrastination to be a liability. A positive strength embedded in procrastination is that delaying provides you an opportunity to consider alternatives, gather more information, and thereby make a better decision, or do a better job.

SELF-AFFIRMATION

One strategy that many find helpful is making affirming statements to yourself, especially when the narcissistic rage statements are cutting, critical, or unfair accusations. Self-affirmations highlight and remind you of your positive attributes, and keep you from agreeing with negative statements made by others. A process for developing these is described in Chapter 10.

FEAR

Fear, terror, and dread are terms used to describe reactions to an expectation of anticipation of destruction or abandonment. The anticipated destruction or abandonment can be either physical or psychological, or both. Fear is a basic emotion that gets transformed and altered in many ways throughout life.

Fear of psychological destruction may be the basis for actions such as the following; attacking others; withdrawing from conflict with those perceived to be powerful; reasonable risk taking, such as making a career change that means additional needed income; any fear of failure; reluctance to enter new situations or have new experiences that have the potential for personal growth; anxiety; etc. Fear of abandonment can be seen in actions or reactions such as jealousy, constantly subjugating personal needs for others, staying in unfulfilling or abusive relationships, inability to be assertive, striving not to be perceived as "different," having to know everything about the other person, being overprotective or seeking protection from others, feeling hopeless or helpless and expecting to be rescued, living by someone else's values with little or no understanding of one's own personal values, working to get constant attention, excessively wanting to please others, dreading being alone, etc. These are but a few examples of how behaviors, attitudes, and feelings are reflections of the two basic fears of destruction and abandonment. These fears begin in infancy, can be modified by life experiences, but for some people, remain in the infantile state throughout their lives.

Children have basic fears about being destroyed and of being abandoned. Themes in many fairy tales address these fears by showing that it is possible to overcome them. Over and over again, a child in these tales is confronted with destruction and abandonment. For example, in Hansel and Gretel, the children face both being taken to the forest by their parents and left alone there, and being potentially destroyed by the witch. However, through their own endeavors they both escape the witch and find their way home. In another story, Little Red Ridinghood faces destruction by the wolf who has eaten her grandmother. Her screams attract the hunter, who kills the wolf and saves both Red Ridinghood and her grandmother. She tried to escape the wolf and called on a more powerful person, to prevent destruction. One final example is Snow White, who was left in a forest, and she did not die there but was rescued by the seven dwarfs, but was once again put in danger of dying by the poisoned apple. Although these fears may be transformed in adults, they do persist into adulthood.

These fears are basic and remain mostly unmodified in adults who have not fully developed healthy narcissism. They remain in their archaic form as experienced in childhood and provide some of the basis for the exhibited behavior. Further, there may also be competing fears. The adult may fear psychological destruction in imtimate relationships, and as a consequence exhibit behaviors designed to prevent intimate relations from developing. However, the same person may also fear abandonment, so he or she is jealous. The targets of these fears receive conflicting messages and are constantly kept off balance, not knowing what to expect. On some days they are expected to get close and reassure that they will not leave, and at other times they are pushed away or frozen out. Little wonder, then, that these are not usually lasting relationships.

It may be helpful to remember that destructive narcissists have ready access to their fears of being destroyed and of being abandoned, which continue to exist in the archaic form experienced in childhood. These fears underlie much of their behavior, attitudes, and feelings and, more important, destructive narcissists usually are not consciously aware of these fears.

Fear can be experienced and expressed in various ways depending on the type of destructive narcissism. Those who fall into the *needy* category can be described as fearing psychological destruction in their incessant demands. They consider themselves incapable of fulfilling their needs, that is, they are helpless, and they face destruction if these needs are not met. The fear of abandonment is seen in their clinging behavior; they fear they will not be able to continue to exist if the other person abandons them.

Those who fall into the *critical* category are not only very fearful of their own destructive capabilities but also fear that others have the intent of destroying them. Thus, they perceive attacks where none was intended and seek to prevent attacks from others by attacking first, or being suspicious, and by criticizing or blaming others. Fear of abandonment is displayed by jealousy, insistence on knowing everything about the other person, and hypersensitivity to perceived rejection.

Those who fall into the *manipulative* category fear that if their mask were ever breached or seen through, the other person would be so enraged at the impostor that they would then be destroyed, rejected, and abandoned. Their lies and deceit are calculated to keep others off guard and at a distance so that they cannot discern the emptiness within.

Those who fall into the *exhibitionistic* category are characterized by arrogance and self-glorification. These people have attained a greater degree of individuation than have those in the other three categories, and are better able to manage their fears. They tend to initiate defenses against the fears, such as leaving the relationship early so as to keep from being abandoned, and going on the offensive so as to keep from being destroyed. They are able to better tolerate their unresolved childhood fears although these fears still have a significant impact on their behavior.

Never forget that the destructive narcissist assumes that you also have these fears, that is, you are not perceived as a separate and distinct individual. Others are also considered to be a potential source of destruction and abandonment and this assumption underlies much of the destructive narcissist's behavior, attitudes, and feelings toward you. For example, destructive narcissists fear abandonment, so they devalue what you have to give them so that they do not have to feel the pain around the loss of something of value, because they are so confident that abandonment will occur.

PERSONAL FEARS

What about your personal fears? How do you exhibit these basic fears in your relationship and interactions with a destructive narcissist? Do you fear the person will abandon you and so try hard to please them to the point where you lose sight of your own needs? Do you fear they will destroy you so you avoid them? Are you less assertive? These are some examples of how fears triggered by the destructive narcissist can impact your behaviors. It may be helpful to reflect on what behaviors you display that are associated with fears of destruction and/or abandonment. Another exercise that may be of benefit is to try and discern when the destructive narcissist is projecting fear onto you and when projective identification is taking place. Once you become aware of projections, projective identifications, and your own issues that trigger the fears leading to identifications, you can begin to take steps to block them and/or modify your reactions.

Fear can have several levels of expression, from a mild discomfort to terror, and sensations and thoughts associated with each level. This information is presented in Table 7.2. Becoming aware of when you are experiencing these levels can provide clues to perceived threats and suggestion strategies to prevent acceleration of fear. This, of course, does not help you understand the antecedents of the basic fears of destruction and/or abandonment. For that kind of understanding, guidance by an experienced and competent therapist is needed; a therapist can also be helpful in effecting long-lasting or permanent change.

What this awareness can do is reveal how and when you transform or disguise your fear, not just to keep others from knowing you are afraid, but to keep yourself unaware of your fear. This unawareness prevents you from feeling

Table 7.2
Levels of Fear and Associated Sensations

Level	Associated Sensations
Discomfort	Vague uneasiness, nervousness, and heightened sense of alarm
Apprehension	Increased alarm, sweating, blushing, and insecurity
Fear	Rapid and shallow breathing, a rush of adrenaline, helplessness, an intensified feeling of inadequacy, and a desire to flee or strike out at a threat
Terror	Panic, paralysis, racing thoughts, very rapid and shallow breathing

a myriad of painful emotions, such as helplessness. However, the more you mute these painful emotions, the more you also blunt the experience of pleasant emotions, such as happiness.

SHAME AND GUILT

Two basic responses to the destructive narcissist are feelings of shame and guilt. These are considered to be different, although they are interrelated. Shame results from the feeling and belief of being flawed and unworthy. The self is so flawed and unworthy that one can never be acceptable, and can never overcome the defects. Guilt, however, refers to feelings that are aroused for failure to live up to expectations. Some fundamental principle was violated. With guilt, the person is not necessarily fatally flawed; he or she just did something wrong. Both shame and guilt develop over time from relationships with the family of origin, the surrounding cultural expectations, and other experiences. The shoulds and oughts transmitted by the family and the culture form the basis for the shame and guilt experienced. Underlying both shame and guilt are fears of abandonment and/or rejection.

Not all shame and guilt are to be avoided. Having these feelings can insure that personal standards are set and met, and your life is lived in accord with your principles. The catch is that many of the standards and principles may have been imposed and incorporated into your being without conscious acceptance. You did not freely choose them and accept them as your values; they just seemed to happen, and you live your life in accordance with them not really knowing that you are doing so. We will discuss these concepts separately.

SHAME

Think of shame as referring to what you are and guilt as a feeling around something you did. These definitions and others point out the importance of shame in self-esteem, self-perceptions, reactions, and relationships with others. The intense reaction to feeling shame is to deny and/or repress it, displace it, or conceal it from others. Denial of feeling shame is a defense against the pain of being flawed and not meeting one's own standards of how you "should" be. When shame is denied and repressed, it goes underground, so to speak, and begins to have influence and an impact in indirect and unconscious ways. Denied and repressed shame retains considerable pain, which one constantly defends against experiencing.

Displaced shame is exemplified in blaming and criticizing behavior, whether it is turned inward against self or outward against others. It may emerge on the unconscious level and be projected onto the other person. An example is seen in what some destructive narcissistic parents do to their children by projecting their shame onto the child, and then react to him or her as being shameful. Unfortunately, the child can then identify with that shame and accept the belief that he or she is shameful.

Concealed shame is probably very common, as almost everyone consciously and unconsciously seeks to hide flaws from others. Considerable defenses are employed to conceal flaws, and the energy used to mount defenses against being found to be imperfect by others can also impact the relationship. It is not so much that the false self is presented as it is that a barrier is put up to prevent revealing the true self. The underlying fear is that if the flaws were seen by others, then the self would be rejected.

IDENTIFYING FEELINGS OF SHAME

Since much shame is unconscious, especially that which is denied and re-pressed, how can you know when your reactions are indicative of shame? Some common feelings that are shame-based or shame-related are embarrassment, humiliation, discouragement, mortification, and remorse. These feelings are reactions to self-perceptions of being flawed, and some are also related to others seeing the flaws. For example, when you experience blame, either self-blame or blame bestowed by someone else, what is your reaction? Do you deny the accusation because to face it means looking at something that is very painful? Or do you feel embarrassed or humiliated that you, or someone else, sees this error or flaw? Do you attack in some way so that the flaw remains hidden, is diluted, or is displaced? These reactions are indicative of shame. Our shame and the way in which we deal with it significantly impacts our relationships with others and on how easily the destructive narcissist is able to trigger shame in us.

Feeling discouraged or depressed is also tied to shame. Shame about not measuring up to the expectations, or of being inadequate, incompetent, and so on, leads to feeling discouraged about your abilities and depressed about yourself. People who feel this way may begin to exaggerate their faults and magnify their blemishes.

Becoming frustrated with yourself is another indication of shame. Frustra-tion develops when attempts appear to fail. For example, you may have worked on not overreacting or personalizing criticism only to find that you do so with the destructive narcissist. You then become frustrated with yourself because you have failed to live up to your expectations of how you will react.

SHAME TRIGGERED BY THE DESTRUCTIVE NARCISSIST

It is very easy for shame to emerge when interacting with destructive narcissists. They usually have powerful projections and others may not have sufficient psychological boundary strength, or self-understanding to prevent identifying with the projection. Thus any insecurity about self-adequacy, self-competence, and one's value can be incorporated and acted on by triggering fears of abandonment and rejection. The receiver is then open to having old parental messages emerge about failing to meet expectations, not being totally acceptable, about being fatally flawed, and these trigger shame for being fatally flawed. It should be remembered that even very experienced therapists can experience these shaming feelings due to the powerful projective identifications of the destructive narcissist, and that they are not always able to protect themselves.

If you also tend to engage in self-shaming behaviors and attitudes, then interacting with this person not only triggers these but can intensify and magnify them. Self-shaming behaviors and attitudes occur when you discount your positive characteristics, magnify your flaws, judge yourself by unrealistic and/or undefined ideals, perceive criticism as focused on what you are rather than what you did, and feel that others are "seeing through you" and know what you are trying to hide, and are contemptuous of you.

STRATEGIES FOR DEALING WITH REACTIONS TO SHAME

The usual reaction when we experience shame is to hide—hide the shaming self from the eyes of others, and hide the shaming self from awareness. Some people may obsess over the shame, returning again and again to the event and the underlying self-statement, and this deepens the pain. Few want to explore the development of their shaming feelings, work through to the point where they understand it, and become able to effectively modify and change it. This is the kind of work done in therapy with a competent therapist and is beyond the scope of what can be presented in this book.

However, there are a few things you can do to deal with your reactions of shame when interacting with a destructive narcissist. Recognition, identification, self-acceptance, and hiding are steps that can aid in dealing with shame. *Recognizing* that your reaction is shame-related is the first step. This can be done by reflecting on the feelings experienced in the interaction. If you found that you wanted to run away, it was probably shame-based. The desire to flee could be exhibited by changing the topic, joking, shifting the focus, or by making an indirect response. Other ways to recognize shame-based feelings occurs when you cringe inside in response to perceived criticism, when you feel that you are being treated like a child and that triggers old childhood responses or feelings, or when you recall old parental messages that speak to your failure or their disappointment with you.

Once you have become aware of or have recognized your shame-based feelings, you can then *identify* old parental messages, and other shaming events that may be triggering these feelings. There is also the possibility that the feelings are a result of projective identification from the destructive narcissist, but even if they are and part of what you are feeling is the projected shame of this person, you have still identified with it and the rest of what you are feeling is your own shame.

Self-acceptance means that you are aware of your shame, and accept that this is a part of your self, but do not blame or reject yourself as a result. This does not mean that you like the perceived flaw, or will not continue to further develop yourself to reduce or eliminate the perceived flaw; it just means that you accept that this is you.

It is not advisable to openly admit your shame to a destructive narcissist, and *hiding* may be the best strategy. Talk to someone whom you trust, begin to continue working with a therapist and/or engage in introspection but do not try to work it out with a destructive narcissist. There are suggestions in many books that it is helpful to stop hiding your shame and it will become less painful and threatening. This may be true, and is certainly true when working with a therapist for self-acceptance, but it may be destructive for you if you become too open with a destructive narcissist. His or her reaction is most likely to be, "Aha, I thought so! You are flawed and I am not. Therefore, what I do or say to you is justifiable." If you protest or suggest that they are not understanding, the likely response is, "But you yourself said you were flawed. I'm only going by what you said." Such a response leads to more feelings of frustration on your part.

Once these steps are accomplished, you will find that while some shame is still attached, it will be less painful and you will feel less threatened by it being known to others. An additional bonus is that the more you can accept yourself with its flaws, the more accepting you can be of others, thus leading to improved relationships. Interactions with the destructive narcissist will be less frustrating because your shame will be lessened and less liable to be expanded by his or her shame, and the impact of old parental messages triggering your shame will be reduced.

One final strategy relates to protecting yourself from the shame-triggering projective identifications until you have achieved self-acceptance, which is not quickly nor easily done. I call the strategy "walling off." It is a form of emotional isolation from the projections of others. Prepare yourself mentally before interactions with the destructive narcissist. I use the visualization of a high steel door in a wall closing me off from the projections. A colleague always mimes pulling down a shade. Use whatever works for you. The idea is that you are aware that this person has powerful projective identifications that can trigger shame in you and that you are consciously trying to shut them off from yourself. My steel doors not only serve to shut them off but also to reflect them back to the destructive narcissist. Since instituting that symbolic walling off, I am better able to tolerate these interactions and do not leave them experiencing shame, or in turmoil, or wondering why I feel as I do. While I do not like being walled off, it has allowed me to maintain my equilibrium.

GUILT

If, in your interactions with a destructive narcissist you find yourself constantly wanting or having to explain, justify, defend, or apologize, then feelings of guilt have most likely been triggered. When you feel guilty, you feel like you are on trial before an unfriendly judge and jury, and it is up to you to present your case. Sometimes you may feel that if the other person could only understand, have all the facts, or see it from your perspective, then he or she would not condemn you. Guilt also occurs when you have erred in some way. You did not act in accord with expectations, rules, laws, or cultural standards. For some, these are shaming experiences, but shame may have an overlay of guilt. It is not easy to separate guilt and shame sometimes, and they may be intertwined.

Guilt, like shame, arises from fears of abandonment and rejection. The difference comes in the actions taken. Guilt can be overcome with confession and atonement; shame is hidden and shut off or denied. In other words, you can take steps to remediate guilt, and there is the possibility that you can receive assurances from others that you will neither be abandoned nor rejected, depending on the offense. Indeed, many religions are constructed around the concept of forgiveness and acceptance after confession and atonement.

Interactions with a destructive narcissist can trigger guilty feelings because this person usually blames others for real or imagined offenses. If they have a need to off-load guilty feelings; shore up a perception of self-adequacy; defend against feelings of abandonment or rejection; or be thought of as flawless, perfect, unique, and special; their projections may trigger your feelings of guilt. Your guilt can occur because you can accept that you err, and you are also willing, on some level, to accept responsibility for your errors. The destructive narcissist is not accepting of his or her errors and will off-load them on to you, and because you realize that you did or could make errors, guilt arises.

The interesting thing is that your efforts to explain, defend, justify, and apologize are reinforcing to the destructive narcissist that he or she was correct in their evaluation of you. Destructive narcissists are not open to hearing explanations nor to accepting any unusual circumstances that apply, etc., but are very willing to accept any apologies because, after all, they had pointed out to you just how wrong you were and your apology acknowledges how correct they were. They brush aside every explanation.

This behavior and attitude can be very frustrating. Here you were trying to accept your responsibility, deal with your feelings of guilt by admitting your part of the error (confessing), and atoning (explaining, justifying, defending, or apologizing), only to meet with a smug reaction of, "I was right, you were wrong." Guilt then becomes tinged with anger or rage. You are not being allowed to atone, but have been found wanting and pushed to remain in your state of guilt. You still have the twin fears of abandonment and rejection.

What would be effective? How can you deal with the guilt feelings aroused in an interaction with the destructive narcissist? You have to respond immediately, and it is extremely difficult to do so in the maelstrom of guilty feelings you are experiencing. Following are some actions that can be helpful, although it may take some time before they become automatic and you do not have to consciously remind yourself to do them.

STRATEGIES FOR COPING WITH GUILT REACTIONS

Do Not Volunteer Explanations

If asked to explain, do so in very concrete, specific terms and not in a tentative way. Just present facts with a minimum of verbiage and do not use nonverbal behavior that conveys an apology, a plea for understanding, or lack of self-confidence.

Why not volunteer an explanation if giving a rationale might lead to understanding? It is very difficult for some people to accept that explaining is perceived by many as defensive behavior and if you feel a need to defend yourself, then you are accepting that you were wrong and that you are guilty. While you may think that you are only clarifying matters, the other person may respond to you as if you are wrong and/or guilty, or that you ought not feel the way they think you feel. For example, have you ever felt you were explaining, only to have the other person respond with words such as, "Don't be so defensive!" That response can generate anger in you because you now feel misunderstood, and do not know what you did to have the other person term you defensive. Waiting until you are asked for an explanation makes it clear that you are responding to a request, not rushing in to defend yourself.

DECREASE DEFENSIVENESS

Make the explanation specific and concrete. Do not overexplain, as this can be perceived as defensive behavior. Put yourself in the position where the other person has to ask for the information he or she wants rather than you trying to guess and thereby overexplaining. It's best if you do not feel defensive, but that takes time to develop.

REFRAIN FROM TRYING TO JUSTIFY YOUR ACTIONS OR POSITION

You are not on trial and do not have to convince the other person of the correctness of what you did or how you feel. If you feel that it is your responsibility to convince others most of the time, then you are tapping into your feelings of guilt springing from fears of being abandoned and rejected. If you can ever accept that you do not have to justify your actions or position all the time, to everyone, you will have done much to address feelings of guilt. Save justifications for those rare cases where it is warranted.

When you feel a need to defend yourself, ask yourself, "Is this defense necessary?" Defense is usually employed against an attack. Could it be that you feel attacked? If so, it may be more productive to explore the notion that you are being attacked, which is what it is that makes you feel attacked; to deflect the attack; or to ignore the attacking behavior. You do not have to engage because you are being attacked, even if you are unfairly attacked.

There may be no need to defend because the defense is coming as a response to an internal perception of attack rather than from an actual attack. You may feel attacked because of your issues, not because the other person intended or set out to attack. For example, some people feel attacked when others ask them questions, when the intent was to gather information or to show interest. This perception has happened on two different occasions in my group counseling classes; student questioning produced reported feelings of being attacked in fellow students whose stated intents were to show interest. Becoming aware of these reactions and perceptions helped me and my students understand that others can feel attacked when there was no intent to attack.

APOLOGIZE WHEN IT IS CALLED FOR, BUT DO NOT RUSH TO DO SO

Wait until you are sure what the nature of the offense is so that you do not apologize for the wrong thing and so that it can be accepted by the other for the perceived offense. In other words, do not apologize for what you would have perceived as offensive; apologize for what the other person considers to be offensive.

It will take practice, but try not to overapologize. Be sincere but not too effusive. Say your piece and let it go. Do not continue to apologize or bring the subject up again. If the apology does not seem to satisfy the other person, wait until he or she has had time to regroup before reintroducing the topic. You have already apologized, and if the person needs a few days to deal with feelings and accept your good-faith apology, do provide that space. Continuing to force your apology on the person is meeting your need, not theirs.

If you must or feel the need to apologize to a destructive narcissist, try to do so when you two are alone, make it short and do not linger to discuss it or anything else. Extending an apology when others are present can intensify the DNP's need for attention, sense of grandiosity, their need to feel unique and special, and/or their sense of entitlement. They may "play to the audience" and use your apology to enhance themselves by discounting or denigrating you. After all, you are admitting in public that you were wrong. You may leave feeling worse than you did before you apologized.

SUMMARY

Intense and negative feelings are uncomfortable and can be distressing. These can be easily and often triggered in interactions with destructive narcissists, but these are your feelings and you are not "made" to have them. It is not helpful or constructive to think that others make you feel as you do, and thinking so aids destructive narcissists because you then are not able to employ more helpful and constructive strategies in interactions with them. You can help yourself to not react and carry the intense negative feelings that can be aroused in interactions with destructive narcissists.

CHAPTER 8

The DNP in Relationships

This chapter focuses on describing the impact of a Destructive Narcissistic Pattern on significant relationships. Presented are: identifying the person with a DNP in the work setting, parental destructive narcissism, and the DNP in intimate relationships. Also presented are some basic assumptions that guide suggested strategies. Specific coping strategies are presented in the next chapter.

THE DNP IN THE WORK SETTING

There are few jobs where you do not have to deal with coworkers and bosses and the quality of these relationships can be a source of interpersonal job stress. Stress comes from unfair and inconsiderate supervisors and bosses, a lack of trust for coworkers and/or boss, feelings of being unrecognized or unappreciated, and being subjected to conflicts. These stressors affect other parts of one's life, and other relationships. Frustrations with a repressive work environment are often displaced on the family in direct and indirect ways, thereby also affecting the quality of family life and other relationships.

The effects of working with destructive narcissists are also felt on the job. For example, job stress costs American industry more that $150 billion a year, or more, in absenteeism, lost productivity, accidents, and medical insurance. While not all job stress results from having to work with someone who has a DNP, the identification of interpersonal relationships as a major job stressor indicates that this situation could well be related with one such outcome. The list of healthy job characteristics, and how the boss or coworker with a DNP

Table 8.1
DNP Behaviors That Reduce Healthy Job Characteristics

Characteristics of Healthy Jobs	Boss's Behavior	Colleague Behaviors
Skill discretion	Orders, micromanaging	Orders without authority
Autonomy	Orders, micromanages, violates boundaries, criticizes	Violates boundaries, criticizes, refuses to admit culpability
Psychological demands	Gives confusing instructions, misleading directions, and orders	Distorts, lies, makes misleading statements
Social relations	Finds faults, makes disparaging and devaluing remarks	Lack of trust, assumes undue credit, makes disparaging remarks
Social rights	Confrontation ineffective, blames	Confrontation and compromises are ineffective, blames
Meaningfulness	Little or no positive feedback, criticizes, and blames	Off-loads responsibility and blame

behaves that circumvents achievement of the characteristic is presented in Table 8.1.

IDENTIFYING THE COLLEAGUE WITH A DNP

The colleague who has a DNP is very difficult to detect, and this person can do you considerable harm with the boss and others in power, because he or she is not recognized as having a DNP. Other colleagues usually recognize that this person is destructive, though terms other than destructive narcissism are used to describe the person. Indeed, one way you can be sure you are dealing with someone with a DNP is through the similarities in the experiences and reactions of your colleagues to this person who describe him or her as frustrating, deceptive, self-aggrandizing, pushy, and other negative descriptors.

To identify a colleague as having DNP read the following list of behaviors and attitudes. If he or she does several of the following actions consistently over time in relations with you and other colleagues, then you are likely working with someone who has a DNP.

- *Makes devaluing or disparaging comments about you to the boss or supervisor.* It does not seem to matter what the occasion is; the person finds a way to devalue you and your work, especially to the boss or the supervisor, often in your presence or behind your back. Off-the-wall nasty comments are also common. These are usually very subtle and tacked on to a more positive statement so that it is difficult to challenge or charge the person with being negative. The pattern of behavior is very difficult to recognize at first.

- *Takes credit for others' work and/or ideas.* It is extremely difficult to overcome credit-taking behaviors after they occur. There are few things that are more infuriating than the realization that someone is taking credit for your work or ideas. Not only is this unfair, but these people can be negatively influencing and impacting your reputation, and your work related rewards, such as raises and promotions. Trying to correct this "lie" can be very time consuming and, in some cases, futile. Even when this person cooperates in correcting the error, they make it appear that you are in the wrong.

- *Boasts and brags constantly.* The destructive narcissist would probably term this behavior as "letting you know what they are doing." This would not be difficult to accept at face value if they were also accepting of the accomplishments of others. However, they only want to hear about themselves.

- *Gives orders to colleagues and expects them to obey.* This is one of the more annoying habits and is one way that destructive narcissists get others to do their work. They phrase it in a way to make it appear that they are passing on a message from the boss. You only learn later that you did their work and that they are taking credit for it.

- *Expects you to do personal favors.* Those with a DNP always expect you to do personal favors, but do few or none in return, and have some excuse as to why they cannot do a favor for someone.

- *Does not respect boundaries.* The destructive narcissist as a colleague will borrow or take others' possessions without asking, enter offices or spaces of colleagues without knocking or asking, and interrupt conversations at will.

- *Does not listen to colleagues.* The destructive narcissist neither solicits nor is tolerant of input from others. When forced to listen to others' input, will find some way to discount the input and the person.

- *Has all the answers.* Whatever the topic, the person not only has all the answers but also knows what is best or right.
- *Lies.* Destructive narcissists lie about inconsequential things, mislead, give you information they know to be inaccurate, etc.

THE SUPERVISOR OR BOSS WITH A DNP

One of the most uncomfortable circumstances to find yourself in is having a supervisor or boss who has a DNP. It may take some time before you accept that he or she has these characteristics, and once you do, it becomes even more frustrating because there seems to be little you can do to protect yourself from increasing frustration, anger, despair, and helplessness. Even if you have the option of leaving, making sufficient arrangements to do so takes time, and in the meantime you still have to experience all the negative aspects of working with him or her.

How can you identify the supervisor or boss who has a DNP? The following list provides some indicators. Many are the same as for the colleague, but may carry more importance since the boss directly affects your raises, job advances, and/or job security. Read this list and see if your boss has a significant number of these behaviors and attitudes.

- Devalues you and your work, ideas, and so forth
- Takes credit for your work and ideas
- Expects you to do favors for him or her
- Blames you and others for their errors
- Boasts, brags
- Micromanages
- Lies, misleads, and distorts information
- Gives confusing instructions
- Criticizes, makes unwarranted charges, attacks without provocation
- Is hypersensitive to perceived criticism
- Is hypercritical—nothing anyone does is right or enough
- Discourages ideas and opinions from others
- Inflates his or her accomplishments
- Is suspicious and mistrustful
- Is resentful

- Feels that only his or her ideas have merit
- Does not empathize

WHY THE COLLEAGUE OR BOSS WITH A DNP GOES UNIDENTIFIED

One of the recurring questions that people ask is why supervisors and bosses do not accept reports of behavior and recognize or understand what the colleague with a DNP is doing that has such a negative impact. If you have a destructive narcissist colleague, you have probably questioned and discussed with others some frustrations and the destructive narcissist's behavior that everyone is sure that the boss must know. But the boss does not seem to understand and is certainly not doing anything about it. There are several possibilities for the failure to recognize or understand the negative impact of the destructive narcissist. Remember that this person is usually intelligent, has some competencies, and is adept at manipulation. Some other possibilities follow.

Similarities. There are two possibilities under similarities; one is that the boss himself or herself has the same characteristics as the person identified as having DNP, and the other is that this person mirrors those characteristics of the boss's of which the boss is most self-accepting. The first possibility gains some credence, because we are attracted to those we find almost similar to ourselves in some important way. Management and organizational studies point out that one of the ways to succeed in organizations is to be similar to those in power. So it is logical that when the destructive narcissist and the boss have similar characteristics, such as being the center of attention, the boss is unable to perceive this characteristic as troubling to others.

The second possibility is also logical. We usually have some characteristics that we like about ourselves, and when others have, or seem to have, the same characteristics, then we would appreciate that characteristic in others as long as we did not feel threatened by it. If we were the boss we would tend to see the ambitiousness of the destructive narcissist as similar to ours and admire him or her for it.

Powerful projections. The person with a DNP usually has powerful projections. While colleagues will experience the more negative ones, the boss will experience positive projections. For example, where the destructive narcissist projects anger onto you and reacts to you as if you were angry when you are not, he or she will project acceptance, approval, warmth, and caring onto the boss and react accordingly. This means that the boss only gets positive vibes from this person, and the general reaction to positive vibes from others is favorable.

Grandiosity as confidence. Another possibility is that the boss misinterprets the grandiosity of the destructive narcissist as self-confidence. This is very easy to do, as most people do not usually think of perceiving people in terms of their grandiosity. It is only over time that you come to understand that a person is exhibiting grandiosity. This is the person who tells the boss that he or she can do a job for which he or she is not qualified, gets the job, and finds ways to blame his or her colleagues for the failures.

Lack of emotions. Many destructive narcissists usually have shallow emotions, and this means that they tend not to be emotionally expressive. That is, they neither have nor express a wide range or intensity of emotions. Supervisors and bosses tend to be reluctant to deal with emotions. They tend to value detachment, which is often referred to as a "professional manner or attitude." Being objective, emotionally detached, and not showing feelings openly makes it easier for bosses and supervisors to deal with employees.

Flattery. Bosses and supervisors are not immune to being misled by flattery. The fact that the flattery is insincere does not appear to make a difference, as the person with a DNP is very adept at masking deceit. These people take every opportunity to flatter the boss or supervisor, and let the boss or supervisor know that they feel that they are wonderful. There are very few people who do not have a positive response to those who tell them they are wonderful.

Off-loading blame. As noted in other chapters, the destructive narcissist is extremely skillful at off-loading blame. These people do not accept blame from anyone, and when faced with mistakes, errors, fraud, etc., manage to convince others that they are faultless and that someone else is to blame. They point to where others made errors in the past, implying that others must be responsible this time also. It's never their mistake, it was someone else's mistake that led to their not being entirely perfect.

BASIC ASSUMPTIONS

There are six assumptions to guide your understanding of the workplace destructive narcissist.

- Challenging the person or complaining about him or her is not constructive for your well-being, or for the positive perceptions of others.
- You and others will be misled by their charming ways at first, and some people will remain under their spell. Their negative acts and attitudes will be rationalized by these people.

- The negative effects of destructive narcissists will be most intense on their co-workers, and they are unlikely to identify what is being done and said that produces the negativity. The unit or team will suffer from reduced productivity and cohesion.

- The boss or supervisor will likely not recognize the destructive narcissist as such.

- You must accept that your usual coping strategies are not effective and will not be effective with this person.

- You cannot relate to them on an adult-to-adult basis (remember the ticked off baby).

There are some fundamental assumptions and actions that are counterproductive with a destructive narcissist, although these may be a part of your characteristic way of interacting with others and/or resolving conflicts. For the most part, your characteristic ways of interacting and conflict resolution will not work effectively with someone who has a DNP. The first step is recognizing and accepting that you must use different coping strategies with the DNP. The tendency is to use and stick with whatever worked for you in the past even though you may have ample evidence that what you are doing is not effecting any change in the other person, uncomfortable feelings continue to be triggered for you, and the relationship is not improved.

Second, those with a DNP are stuck in psychological development somewhere between infancy and late childhood, although they are physically adults. You cannot expect them to react and behave as adults. They give the appearance of being adults and because you are unlikely to be able to determine the stage of psychological development in which they are stuck, you have certain assumptions about their behavior and attitudes. It will be less frustrating if you accept that they are not adults psychologically and that you cannot relate to them on an adult-to-adult basis. You do not have to identify their level or stage of psychological development in order to cope; just recognize that they are not truly adults.

The third basic assumption relates to their characteristic of lack of empathy. It is difficult for most of us to accept that destructive narcissists cannot empathize. Although they mask their lack of empathy with correct words, they are not feeling the emotions. It is only over time that you become aware that the words are correct, but there are no feelings behind the words. It is this characteristic that provides the destructive narcissist with protective detachment. They truly do not know, or care, what you feel, nor do they realize or care about the impact of their behavior on others. They assume that everyone is like them, with emptiness within, a shallow emotional life, a sense of entitlement and grandiosity, and others are expected to meet their needs. Trying to empathize or connect with a destructive narcissist by understanding their feelings is futile. Expecting them to understand your feelings or the impact of their behavior on you or expecting them to empathize is also futile. Give up this expectation that has probably worked for you in the past—it will not work this time.

Most adults use confronting or compromising as their primary modes for conflict resolution with adults. In confronting, you invite the other person to examine his or her behavior and its impact on you. By doing so, you expect the other person to care about your feelings and to want to preserve the relationship. Both expectations are wrong in connection with the person with DNP. The destructive narcissist does not care about you or about the relationship. Compromising means that both of you want to resolve the conflict, are willing to try to understand each other's position, and are willing to give up something to resolve the conflict and maintain the relationship. The destructive narcissist does not care about any of this. They are not willing to concede anything to resolve the conflict, nor do they care about preserving the relationship. So do not use either confronting or compromising as conflict resolution strategies.

These basic assumptions set a framework for discussing some things you can do that will be effective in the short-term. Additional and specific strategies can be found in Chapter 9. The other side of coping with the destructive narcissist is that you want to preserve your sense of integrity, self-confidence, or self-esteem, and your feelings of empowerment, that is, the sense that you have some control over what happens to you. Review the following strategies, keeping in mind your personality. Select those that best fit you, but also be open to experimenting with some that seem foreign to you but may be useful in this particular situation.

BASIC STRATEGIES

The three basic strategies are to establish firm clear boundaries, institute emotional insulation, and use cognitive defenses. Your personality will determine how you choose to use these strategies but some form of each of them will enable you to more effectively cope with a destructive narcissist in the workplace.

Establish boundaries. Boundaries refer to both physical and psychological demarcations of self. The destructive narcissist has very poor boundaries, and tends not to recognize the boundaries of other people. People with DNP are stuck in the psychological stage of growth where everything and everyone is an extension of self, and therefore under their control. They tend to be controlling, arrogant, and have an attitude of "my way or the highway." They give orders and expect to be obeyed, do not tolerate questions or suggestions from others, appropriate others' ideas and present them as his or her own, and so forth. Once you realize and accept that the person has a DNP, and is exhibiting these behaviors and attitudes, you can begin to better define your boundaries. You can decide what is most important for you and use that as a guide for your behavior. For example, if the person is controlling, micro-managing, showing a lack of respect for your abilities, devaluing your efforts, and so forth, you can limit your face-to-face interactions. If you are in a work setting, a useful strategy for micromanaging is to request all directions in writing. If the person wants you to do something in a particular way, ask for written directions so that you reduce any possibility of a mistake. Conversely, make your requests to the destructive narcissist in writing. Eliminate impromptu conversations, and if the person stops you and has one that relates to what you are doing, write it up in a memo and promptly send it to the person. An additional point in boundaries and writing memos: use titles. Do not address the person by the first name or sign your first name. Use Mr., Mrs., Ms., Dr., and so forth. Cultivate formality.

Do not give favors or request favors. Do not borrow anything including small items such as pen, paper, or staples. Do not lend anything. Preserve your boundaries and respect the destructive narcissist's boundaries. They will not return the respect, but you did not expect them to do so.

If the person cannot tolerate questions or suggestions, do not ask or make them. If you have questions that relate to clarification of expectations for what you are doing, ask them in a memo with a statement that you are asking for clarification to reduce the possibility of making errors. Make suggestions in writing, with copies to appropriate people. You accomplish two things: you convey your ideas to everyone, and you reduce the possibility that the destructive narcissist will take credit for your ideas.

Emotional insulation. Your feelings of frustration, anger, helplessness, pow-erlessness, and other distressing feelings, are easily triggered by a destructive narcissist if you do not consciously insulate yourself. You will probably experi-ence powerful unconscious projections from the person with a DNP, and the extent to which you identify with these projections, and your unresolved is-sues, and unfinished business determine the level and intensity of the feelings you experience. For example, your own self-doubt about your competency can be triggered by the destructive narcissist's projection of his or her self-doubt. What has happened is that the destructive narcissist's self-doubt has been off-loaded onto you, your existing self-doubt was triggered and expanded to include what was projected, leading to your feelings of anger, helplessness, and so forth.

However, these feelings and identifications will not get triggered if you emotionally insulate yourself. These reactions usually occur in face-to-face interactions, so if you can consciously prepare for these interactions by providing yourself with some insulation, the projections will not get through and trigger your identifications.

How can you emotionally insulate yourself? When I decided I needed to emotionally insulate myself, I visualized a set of steel doors closing between me and the destructive narcissist prior to beginning a conversation, and tried to avoid impromptu conversations. I have a colleague who mimes pulling down a shade before he talks with a destructive narcissist. Another colleague thinks of a brick wall between himself and this person. All of these techniques work for us because we consciously seek to defend ourselves, and this awareness promotes insulation. Develop your own conscious mode of insulation designed to protect yourself from the person with DNP projections and projective identifications. Further, knowing that the uncomfortable feelings are partially yours and were triggered by this person helps you take responsibility for your issues and work on them.

Cognitive defenses. The final set of strategies can be classified as cognitive defenses. They are all designed to help you to "go to your head" when dealing with a DNP instead of having only emotional responses, usually uncomfortable emotional responses.

When you feel yourself becoming frustrated, angry, and so forth, consciously step back and tell yourself that you do not have to feel this way. You are frustrated or angry because of some perceived threat (the usual reactions to threats to the self), but that this is not the time or place to allow yourself to feel this way or to explore the source of the threat. You can do that later.

You can ask yourself, "What's happening with me? Do I have to respond this way?" These are intellectualizations, which are cognitive defenses. Other helpful questions include, "What is he or she trying to do?" and "Is this another manifestation of destructive narcissism?"

The main points are that you cannot change those with a DNP; you can only change your responses to them.

PARENTAL DESTRUCTIVE NARCISSISM

As distressing as it can be to have to work with or for someone who has a DNP, it is more difficult and distressing to have to live with that person. The parent who has many of the characteristics of a DNP has a far-reaching impact on the quality of the relationship—usually a negative impact. This is the person who:

- Expects others to assume responsibility for their emotional and/or physical well-being. This is particularly devastating to the psychological growth and development of a child when he or she is made to be responsible for the mother's or father's well-being. Few relationships flourish well under this condition. They may persist in the relationship, but are not satisfying to either person.

- Belittles and devalues others' efforts. This person can always find a flaw, nothing anyone does is ever adequate, and they are very willing to let others know that their expectations have not been met.

- Seeks to direct others' lives in almost everything—selects their clothes, chooses their friends, tells them what they can and cannot do in even the smallest detail. Although some guidance for children is necessary, the parent with a DNP tries to manage details of children's lives.

- Considers the child to be an extension of himself or herself. Some destructive narcissists name their children a variation of their name or Junior, do not respect others' possessions but feel free to search and use them and invade others' space without minimum courtesy, such as, entering a child's room without knocking.

- Makes unflattering comparisons between their and others' children, spouses, or lovers.

- Takes every opportunity to let others know they are flawed and do not measure up to expectations.

- Is hypersensitive to perceived criticism. Cannot tolerate anyone perceiving them as less than perfect.

- Does things that are designed to result in admiration from others, especially those outside the relationship.

- Does not empathize. Those with a DNP appear unaware and uncaring of the impact of their behavior on those closest to them. When the child tries to let the person know how he or she feels, the destructive narcissist turns it around to make the child appear to be overly sensitive, unable to face facts, and inconsiderate of the parent's feelings. The person is very adept at this kind of manipulation.

- Exhibits characteristics of the boss or colleague with a DNP, such as, boasting, bragging, attacking, blaming, lying, having all the answers, giving orders and expecting them to be obeyed, and discouraging input from others.

Parental destructive narcissism is exhibited in a couple of ways: the parent(s) has a chronic inability to empathically respond to the infant. The chronic inability is usually due to some disturbance or pathology in the parent, such as depression or pathological narcissism. another situation is when children are thrust into the role of caretakers for parents who are emotionally and sometimes physically unable to care for themselves. Children then become the nurturers instead of the parents.

In either case, the parent does not act as a parent, nurturing and caring for the child, and because of this deficit or neglect, the child fails to receive empathic responses. The destructive narcissism of the parent has a negative impact on the healthy development of narcissism for the child. The child is reinforced for those responses that meet the undeveloped narcissistic needs of the parent with a DNP instead of the parent meeting the needs of the child. The results play out in numerous ways that follow the person throughout his or her life. Some examples of the impact of having a parent with a DNP follow.

Responsibility for parental well-being. When children have to assume responsibility for the parent's well-being, they may find themselves assuming this role for others throughout their lives. These are the individuals who are overly responsible or those who cannot be induced to meet anyone's needs. They either respond to emotional blackmail or they become defiant at the slightest hint that someone is counting on them for emotional well-being. There does not appear to be an in between response.

Parents who have a DNP cannot nurture because they are not at the level where they can consider *the infant as separate and distinct* from themselves. The infant is an extension of self, produced by them, and thus must meet their needs. This attitude is played out throughout the child's life, where the child is approved of only when meeting the parent's narcissistic need. For example, if the destructive narcissistic parent has a need to be the center of attention, then he or she expects the child to perform so that the parent will be the center of attention. The parent feels that the child's accomplishments are due to the parent's efforts or even to the parent's existence. In other words, all attention is due to the parent, with little or none for the child.

Belittling and devaluing. Parents with a DNP take every opportunity to belittle and devalue the child. They speak often of how the child is flawed, inadequate, disappointing to the parent, and so forth. If challenged, they speak of having high standards, but fail to see that no one could possibly meet these standards. This characteristic is one that builds shame in the child. Children end up feeling so fatally flawed that they know at the core of their being that they can never be adequate. This is a feeling that underlies much shame and contributes to low self-esteem. Sometimes when parents think that they are helping the child, they are really trying to get the child to meet their own destructive narcissistic needs.

Micromanaging the child. Some parents with a DNP tend to micromanage their children. Sometimes it is difficult to know when one is being sufficiently supportive and when one is being overprotective, overbearing, meddling, or micromanaging. Many parents err on the side of caution, feeling that it is better to make sure the child receives sufficient support rather than not enough. This is not micromanaging.

Micromanaging occurs when the child is told what to do, how to do it, when to do it almost all of the time, and/or when the parent constantly monitors the child. They are constantly disapproved of if they do not meet the stated and unstated standards of the parents. Destructive narcissistic parents, because they consider the child to be an extension of self, expect the child to know what they want, and to give them what they want at all times, can become angry when the unstated needs are not met, and blames the child for not reading their minds.

The child as an extension of the parent. All parents feel a sense of pride when their children do something well or something that is difficult, such as, attain good grades in school or do well in sports, music, or dance. However, some parents go to extremes in their attitudes when they consider the child to be an extension of self. The child is not perceived as separate and distinct, but as a part of the parent, and their accomplishments are solely or mainly due to the parent. Thus, the child exists only to gratify the parent and is under the parent's control. All of this is taking place on a nonconscious level and the parent is not aware of his or her attitude or unconscious assumption. Because children do need help, nurturing, and protection, these parents, if confronted about their attitude, would respond that they are only trying to take care of their children.

When parents have this attitude, they do not foster the expected psychological development stage of separating or individuating. Sometimes a child will struggle to separate and individuate in spite of the parent's attitude, but it is unlikely to become a lifelong struggle that may never be fully completed. The child as an adult will find that he or she carries traces of uncompleted separation and individuation throughout life. This, in turn, can contribute to incomplete or destructive narcissism in the person.

Comparison with others. The parent with a DNP may feel that comparisons with their children, either between siblings, with other family members, or with those outside the family, will inspire, or motivate a child, or increase understanding of parental expectations. Whatever their assumptions or beliefs, when parents make comparisons, the usual results are not what were intended. Comparisons tend to promote resentment, defiance, envy, jealousy, self-denigration, and an erosion of self-confidence, and self-esteem. Although some children may increase efforts to please the destructive narcissistic parent, the parent's comparisons negatively impact the child's perception of his or her self-worth.

These effects are also carried into adult life, where they continue to have a significant impact on behaviors, attitudes, and relationships. For example, the person who has difficulty with authority figures, the person who constantly sacrifices needs in favor of satisfying others, and the person who rebels against expectations could be manifesting the results of a parental DNP's comparison with others. Worse yet is the situation where the parental DNP's behavior and attitude are internalized and acted out, so that when the children become adults they then do the same to their children.

Hypersensitivity to perceived criticism. When parents with a DNP are hypersensitive to perceived criticism, their children suffer if they say anything that the parent considers criticism, if they exhibit any nonverbal behavior the parent takes it as rebuff or criticism, and if anyone else does or says anything they find it offensive. It does not seem to matter that no criticism was intended; if the parent felt criticized, then the other person was being critical of him or her, and even more important, the parent feels the criticism is undeserved.

The impact of this hypersensitivity and displacement can have a significant impact on the child. Children want to please their parents, and when they are faced with a parent's displeasure children can internalize the displeasure and incorporate a message that they are bad, flawed, or wrong. This message then becomes a part of the self and impacts their self-esteem.

Another impact of this hypersensitivity is that the child grows up never knowing or understanding what triggers the hypersensitivity to perceived criticism. The parent with a DNP does not become less prone to hypersensitivity over time, but appears to seek out and react to more perceived nuances of criticism. Sometimes it may seem that almost everything is perceived as criticism. This uncertainty can unconsciously influence the child's relationship throughout life.

Admiration-seeking behavior. Parents with a DNP expect their children to perform and to act in a way that bestows admiration upon the parent. The child is not a distinct, separate person but is an extension of the parent. These are the parents who seem to others to live through their children, in many ways. We have all heard of the "stage mother" who manages her child so that she, the mother, is recognized, and the father who demands that his child excel in sports. Entering children in beauty contests, having young children leave home to work with coaches for the Olympics or other events, insisting that children take lessons in anything so that they can outperform others, whether or not this is of interest to the child, are examples of parents pushing children.

Some of these activities are meant to bring recognition and admiration to the parent and can be detrimental to the child in indirect and long-lasting ways.

There is a vast difference between providing children with opportunities to learn and excel in an activity, such as dance, baseball, drama, and art, and insisting that a child participate, learn, and/or excel because of the reflected glory it brings to the parent. There is considerable agreement about the helpfulness of parental involvement and encouragement in the growth and development of the child. It can be difficult to know when the line has been crossed between encouraging behavior and demanding behavior. However, if the need, desire, or dream being fulfilled or acted out by the child really belongs to the parent, the line has been crossed. If the parent cannot give credit for performing or accomplishment to the child but feels and accepts that the parent is admired, then the parent is engaging in admiration-seeking behavior.

Lack of empathy. When the destructive narcissist does not empathize with his or her child, the child will probably have one or more reactions that set the pattern of expectations and interactions throughout life. Some reactions in children are a restriction or blocking of feelings, reluctance, or inability to trust their feelings, focusing on others' feelings and discounting their own, and/or an erosion of self-confidence. The child, by example, does not learn to empathize.

As noted before, many with a DNP have a shallow emotional life and an inability to empathize with others. Thus, these parents probably do not recognize the level, intensity, and variety of emotions in the child; nor are they able to understand what the child is feeling. This side of human existence is not available to them. While they are able to identify sensations, they cannot access emotion in themselves, making them blind to the emotions of others.

This lack of empathy is one of the characteristics of healthy narcissism in an adult. Parents who cannot or, do not, empathize with their children are modeling destructive narcissism. For example, a parent charges the child with a transgression, the child protests and denies the charge, the parent does not empathize or even consider that the child may be correct, and goes on to berate the child about additional concerns, such as lack of respect for the parent. The child is put in the position of being wrong no matter what he or she says or does. Never forget that these parents do not see their behaviors and attitudes as needing change.

It is not unreasonable to expect parents to be empathic, not always empathic but mostly so. It is also reasonable to expect a parent to value their children as worthwhile, unique individuals. That is not to say that the parent should always agree with their children or approve of their actions, but children should be able to expect that their parents will have an underlying sense of valuing and respecting them.

THE SIGNIFICANT OTHER WITH A DNP

The early stage. It is easy to become enthralled with someone who has a DNP, as he or she can be very charming and attentive. Many with a DNP are usually lively and outgoing, and able to talk easily with others. At first they are also enthralled with you and believe that you are the person who can fulfill their needs and dissipate the emptiness within. And so they hang on your every word, flatter you, desire to be with you, and do everything to make you believe you are important to them and their well-being.

The disillusion stage. It is only after some tine that you realize that the person is no longer enthralled with you. By that time you may either be married or have a significant emotional commitment to the relationship, as you love and care for the person. You probably increase your efforts to please him or her and become increasingly frustrated when nothing works; you begin to have self-doubts and do a lot of self-blaming.

Challenging stage, truing to recapture the early stage. If you were to analyze the course of the relationship, you would probably discover that signs of a DNP were present but not identified. The person had a history of failed relationships as evidenced by numerous marriages that ended in divorce, or other intimate relationships that broke up after a somewhat short period. The person will have demonstrated over and over that he or she is unable to develop and maintain satisfying relationships.

Other characteristics that may have been present early in the relationship are the desire to be admired, the need to be the center of attention, and to be considered unique and special, and/or the feeling that rules, laws, and so forth do not apply to them. You may have been willing to be all-admiring at first, seeing no faults. Rose-colored glasses do have their advantages. However, there does come a time when reality begins to creep in, and while you still consider the person to be wonderful, you are able to see faults and still be accepting and caring.

Reality Stage. More corrosive to the relationship are the person's attitudes and behaviors of criticizing and off-loading blame, making misleading and distorted statements, or even constantly lying, and lack of empathy. Gradually you realize that you are no longer wonderful in their eyes and that your partner is constantly criticizing and blaming you, refusing to accept any responsibility for maintaining the relationship, making demeaning and devaluing remarks to you, expecting you to show concern for him or her with none shown to you in return, and not empathizing no matter how much empathy you give.

You may try some form of confronting where you bring to the person's attention his or her behavior and its impact on you and the relationship. There is little or no success in doing this, as no significant changes happen, and you always feel worse. Self-doubt increases, anger and frustration flare up, and you may even feel that you are in a hopeless situation and are helpless. The pattern may become chronic but also have periods when it is acute.

After the challenging stage does not bring about desired changes, there seem to be two responses; either you or your partner decide to sever the relationship, or your change in an effort to meet his or her needs.

A complicating factor is that your underdeveloped narcissism can be more easily triggered in intimate relationships. This is akin to adding fuel to the fire. Interactions may become more like children's fights with each other than like adult interactions, where each person is making some good-faith effort to understand the other person. As much of this is not conscious on either person's part, neither is aware of what is happening, and so the conflict and disagreeable feelings increase and may escalate.

CHAPTER 9

Moderating the Impact of the DNP on You

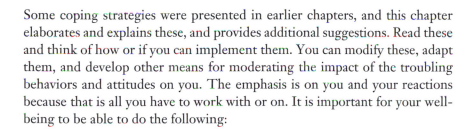

Some coping strategies were presented in earlier chapters, and this chapter elaborates and explains these, and provides additional suggestions. Read these and think of how or if you can implement them. You can modify these, adapt them, and develop other means for moderating the impact of the troubling behaviors and attitudes on you. The emphasis is on you and your reactions because that is all you have to work with or on. It is important for your well-being to be able to do the following:

- Relinquish the fantasy that the destructive narcissist will change because you want him or her to, or believe that change is in his or her best interest. They can change, but only when they decide to do so.

- Give up the yearning you have for the connections, intimacy, acceptance, and approval from the destructive narcissist. These too are probably fantasies, or futile wishes that prevent you from effectively coping and building yourself.

- Do not confront this person. The destructive narcissist can be deeply wounded by confrontation, thereby triggering his or her narcissistic rage. People with a DNP cannot be objective and rational in a confrontation, they can only defend the self they feel is being attacked.

- Do not give this book to someone, or leave it lying around in the hope that he or she will read it, recognize their troubling behaviors and attitudes, and change. These people seldom, if ever, recognize themselves in these descriptions. They do not see any need to change.

If you can do these things, you can be well along in developing coping skills, and in moderating the impact of their behaviors and attitudes on you.

Moderating the impact involves the following:

- Block identification with their projections by understanding your non-conscious and unconscious old parental messages that you incorporated from birth, and that continue to influence your self-perceptions, self-confidence, and self-esteem.
- Understand your cognitive distortions, such as the need to be perfect, or that you are responsible for the well-being of capable adults.
- Use emotional insulation.
- Do not empathize as this opens you to incorporating their projections, and you run the risk of identifying with these.

Suggested strategies are provided for the four types: needy, critical, manipulative, and exhibitionistic; and for categories of relationships: colleagues at work, the boss, parents, and spouses, and lovers or partners. Also discussed are some general strategies that can be helpful in many situations.

This presentation looks at one's internal resources, associations, parental messages, and cognitive distortions as ways of understanding the impact of the destructive narcissist on oneself and developing responses in accord with one's own needs. The emphasis is on self-understanding, not on the person with a DNP.

BLOCK IDENTIFYING WITH PROJECTIONS

One way to reduce the negative and enduring emotions that can result from interactions with the destructive narcissist is to not identify with their projections. When you identify with these, you unconsciously accept their projected feelings, add them to your's, and thereby increase their intensity and negative effects on you. You are not aware that you are cooperating to accept and make these projected feelings a part of you. The steps to effect blocking are introspection, associations, and understanding your old parental messages.

INTROSPECTION

Introspection is the first step. Taking a look at your personal behaviors and attitudes, or feelings to identify those that are not usual, have increased or decreased, or are troubling to you or to others with whom you have important relationships, and looking at the reemergence of old issues are all part of introspection. Realizing that you are dissatisfied with your responses but not blaming yourself can begin the process.

A word about blaming yourself. Many people, especially those who can empathize with others, are prone to feel they are at fault or have in some way failed to be all that they perceived themselves to be. The cycle of dissatisfaction with self—increased efforts to understand the destructive narcissist and/or to empathize, and resulting failure to alter the situation, both of which lead to increased feelings of inadequacy, frustration, etc., returning back to dissatisfaction with self—results in acceleration of withdrawal and despair. It seems that the more effort one puts into the relationship, the more frustration and self-doubt increase. If you have the perception of self that you are responsible for the frustration because of your unresolved issues or incomplete psychological development, you blame yourself.

Perhaps the first step in introspection is to accept that you have limitations and that you are not to blame. This is not to say that the other person is to blame, but to acknowledge that you are contributing to your own distress if you blame yourself. This may be somewhat difficult to do as those people who accept responsibility for their feelings may also accept the idea that they choose to be frustrated, angry, and so forth, and the other person cannot or does not "make" them have these feelings. Basically, this is true. However, if one is not aware of projections and possible projective identifications, both of which are unconscious processes, then one is not aware that what is experienced is both under one's control and not under one's control.

Once you can accept the fact that not only are you not to blame but that you may or do have personal issues that impact and influence your responses, you can begin to explore the extent to which these personal issues contribute to your personal reactions to the destructive narcissist and develop strategies for dealing with your reactions.

Associations

The next step is to identify the associations that connect the introjected identifications. For example, if you identify with the characteristic lack of empathy and become less empathic, what associations can you make with previous experiencing? Was there a time when you were not empathic because of hurt or fear? Is being empathic associated with feelings of betrayal? Do you know from exploration of personal issues that you had a significant reverse self-object experience in childhood, where you were made to feel responsible for a parent or parents' feelings and not empathizing became your way of not being overwhelmed by the emotions of others? (The reverse self-object experience is discussed in more detail in Chapter 3.) These questions and others can illuminate the associations. Once these are identified, you can begin to understand your reactions and subsequent behaviors with respect to the destructive narcissist and with others, for it would be unlikely that others have not felt a lessening of your empathy in interactions with them.

One process for identifying your associations is free association. This can be done with a tape recorder to record your responses or by writing responses. Begin with a feeling, situation, session, or image, and the intent of opening yourself to true responding without reflection or editing. Whatever comes to mind will be spoken or written.

Keeping the feeling, situation, person, or image in mind, write or record everything that emerges as a thought or feeling. Words, phrases, fragments, and so forth, must all be noted. Write or record until the flow of responses ceases or you find yourself thinking in order to come up with a response.

Once the list has been generated, reread, or listen to it. As you read or listen, what other connections emerge? How are the responses, or parts of responses, linked or further associated? The links or associations will usually be from previous relationships and/or time periods. At this point, some understandings will occur. It may be helpful to record or write the understandings and continue to explore more associations. The next section focuses on understanding your associations.

PARENTAL MESSAGES

Some associations may be parental messages that speak of flaws or inadequacies. That is, the destructive narcissist's verbalizations or actions may trigger remembered parental injunctions, feelings, evaluations, etc. that continue to impact the individual and influence his or her functioning and relationships, albeit on an unconscious level.

These are verbal and nonverbal messages sent by parents to children and received, either clearly or with distortions, and introjected. These messages that define how others react to them are one way children begin to develop self-esteem. Kohut (1977) feels that the mirroring of the child's perception of him or herself by parents is one facet of building healthy narcissism. The parent who approves of and delights in the child is mirroring the child's perception of self, that is, "I am lovable," and conveys this through word and deed.

This is also the process by which the child learns what is acceptable and what is not. Embedded in the learning may be the message that the child is flawed, not just the behavior but the essential self, and this is shameful to both the parent and the child. There are many such messages sent by parents verbally and nonverbally, consciously and unconsciously.

One way of knowing if old parental messages are being triggered and reacted to is listening to your feelings when interacting or after interacting with the DNP. If you feel much as you did when you were a child, there are probably old parental messages being reactivated. If you feel patronized, talked down to, impotent, furious, and/or fatally flawed, then there are parental messages being received. This is not to suggest that the destructive narcissist is not doing or saying patronizing things, or blaming, and so forth, but it is your reaction to what they are doing or saying that is indicative of old parental messages and unresolved issues around them. Becoming aware of and continuing to work on these issues can do much to moderate the impact of this person on you.

COGNITIVE DISTORTIONS

Another approach is to look at possible cognitive distortions you may have about yourself and/or others to determine whether they can be modified, leading to less emotional distress. Examples of cognitive distortions include extremism, focusing on the negative, a doom attitude, all-or-nothing thinking, overpersonalization, and "shouldism." Each will be briefly described.

EXTREMISM

Extremism occurs when thinking patterns try to categorize almost everything into polarities, such as good and bad. There is no room or consideration for shades of gray; whatever, it is either black or white. This kind of cognitive distortion makes for very rigid thought and evaluation of self and others. When the destructive narcissist criticizes or blames, extremism causes the person's response to be either he or she is right and I am very wrong, or she or he is wrong and I am right. In either case, communication ceases and emotional distress can occur from resentment or anger at being right but not perceived as such by that person, or shame and humiliation experienced for being wrong.

FOCUSING ON THE NEGATIVE

Another cognitive distortion occurs when you focus only on the negative and overlook or ignore any positive aspect. This is not to suggest that everything is always positive; everything has a negative side, and this should not be discounted. However, a constant focus only on the negative leads to self-fulfilling prophecy—things are bad or miserable.

Anxiety and misery is increased when the cognitive distortion of focusing on the negative is employed during or after interactions with the destructive narcissist. A tendency to select the negative and emphasize or even obsessing about it can accelerate a depressive spiral. Those with a DNP are blaming and critical of others and say or do things to make others feel inadequate, incompetent, and fatally flawed. If the receiver has the cognitive distortion of focusing on the negative, this attitude helps the destructive narcissist by the receiver not only agreeing with the destructive narcissist's evaluation but also adding to it with additional negative thoughts about the self.

A DOOM ATTITUDE

This attitude focuses on the negative but takes it considerably further. It is a cognitive distortion that assumes doom or dire consequences lie around the corner almost always, and should be foremost in one's thoughts. The person does not know what to do to prevent the imagined negative event, and becomes paralyzed at the awful possibilities that may occur. He or she fears doing anything because it may be wrong, fears doing nothing, and thus is left paralyzed, with a strong sense of dread and doom.

People with this attitude worry a lot, but are paralyzed in the sense of taking action. They may be somewhat hysterical otherwise, with lots of talk about the awfulness and the impending dire consequences. They flail around trying to decide what to do, and dump on anyone who will listen to their sense of awfulness and impending doom. A destructive narcissist is very good at expanding and intensifying this cognitive distortion by pushing the person to do something, with the added caveat that whatever he or she does will be wrong; the destructive narcissist knows this, and will also be there to point out how wrong it was and how inadequate the person is.

ALL-OR-NOTHING THINKING

All-or-nothing cognitive distortions describe an individual who speaks and thinks in terms such as always and never. For example, if someone errs, the thought or response would be that the erring person is always wrong—not that he or she made an error this time. This cognitive distortion does not allow for a holistic appraisal of self and of others; it focuses on one specific thing and generalizes to the whole from that one thing.

People with this cognitive distortion also demand perfection in self and in others. There is no in-between, no allowance made for mistakes, no recognition of limitations. The self and others are perceived as flawed or inadequate unless they are perfect. For example, someone who uses this cognitive distortion would not be pleased with birthday gifts unless each and every one was exactly what he or she wanted. The person would focus solely on the part that was not perfect, ignoring all the gifts that were what was wanted. He or she may even say, "I never get what I want," or something similar.

OVERPERSONALIZATION

Perceiving events as personal slights, attacks, or shaming occurs when people feel inadequate and fear that others can see this inadequacy. No matter what is being said or done, this person reacts as though it were a personal slight, put down, or criticism. They generally act as though someone is blaming them, or expecting them to assume responsibility, and they become angry. This cognitive distortion may arise from old parental messages, or other experiences, such as, having the responsibility to see that others' needs are taken care of and receiving the message that you are "bad" if you do not do a good job. An example of this is when you feel you have failed, or ought to take action if a capable adult comments on their discomfort. Another example could be when you think that comments are an indirect means for attacking you.

People who tend to personalize everything will find it very uncomfortable to interact with the destructive narcissist because this person's projections will tap into their feelings and assumptions that the destructive narcissist's feelings are their responsibility, and that they are not doing an adequate job of taking care of this person. The strong parental messages are reactivated, producing profound feelings of inadequacy, incompetence, and self-doubt. This cognitive distortion allows people to beat up themselves more than the person with a DNP does.

"SHOULDISM"

"Shoulds" and "oughts" can be both good and bad. Cultural expectations and values are transmitted and incorporated by the individual to provide directions for acceptable behaviors, and used in that way, they tell the person what is "good" and what is "bad." For example, in most U.S. communities people are taught that one should be polite, and polite behaviors are modeled and taught. The definition of polite may differ from community to community, but everyone in a particular community knows what he or she should do.

However, shoulds and oughts become cognitive distortions when you do not actively select a particular course of action, but only do what you feel should or ought to be done, act contrary to your self-interest most or all the time, and constantly subjugate yourself to take care of others. The person with a DNP triggers and intensifies this cognitive distortion, and you are miserable because you should be able to do whatever is needed, such as take care of the destructive narcissist. This cognitive distortion readily plays into the grandiose and entitlement assumptions of the person with a DNP that others should and must meet their spoken and unspoken needs.

These are but a few of the many cognitive distortions that individuals employ and by doing so provide additional intensity to projections of the person with a DNP. Thus, not only is the destructive narcissist dumping his or her unwanted feelings, but the receiver is also contributing to his or her own misery with cognitive distortions, particularly those that relate to self-worth.

COPING STRATEGIES

Preventive and coping strategies will focus on helping you effectively deal with someone who relates to you and exhibits the behaviors and attitudes of a DNP and these are presented in this chapter. There are two major points that you should always remember: you cannot change the other person and the person is not aware of the impact of his or her behavior on others. These points are difficult to accept, and you may find, upon reflection, that much of your behavior and feelings are based on the faulty assumptions that you can effect changes in others' behavior, or that if others only knew the impact of their behavior on others, they would then change, or that there is no way that they could not know the impact of their behavior on others. The fact that you have had little or no influence to this point has probably either escaped you, or has caused you to increase your efforts. In either case, the person has not changed, but your frustration and self-doubts have increased.

It may be helpful for you to begin by accepting these two points as working hypotheses. Accepting the two points does not mean you are fully committed to them, just that they can be the beginning assumptions that can be changed when evidence points to the need to do so. These points can be of assistance when you become frustrated and can serve as guides for what to do or not to do. It is somewhat arrogant to presume that you can change the other person, *or* that you have the answer for how he or she ought to be, and that the person should change because you want this. The desire to change the other person tends to ignore or discount their freedom to choose. Letting go of the fantasy that you can or should change the other person frees you to accept the person as he or she is, and to practice what you want others to do.

You may be tempted to confront or attack destructive narcissists. Confrontation or attack does not work, as they are blind to their behavior and the attitudes that aroused the negative feelings in you. They cannot accept that they are in any way flawed, and will turn the confrontation or attack back on you. You usually come out on the losing end of a confrontation or attack, as they are well protected from knowing their "flaws." You, being somewhat aware and accepting of your "flaws," are not as well protected, so your shame and guilt are more easily triggered. Confronting usually results in your feeling worse than before.

What can work? There are some strategies that may be helpful for any of the classifications and some that are more specific. The primary general strategy is to become more aware of where you can work to develop healthy adult narcissism, and to reduce and eliminate any age-inappropriate narcissistic behavior and attitudes.

Another general strategy is to increase your awareness of what you are feeling. Learn to tune in to more minor feelings, such as irritation that could escalate into more intense feelings, such as anger. By doing so, you will find it easier to deal with the more minor feeling, and can prevent it from leading to a more intense and more difficult feeling. One way of tuning in is to focus on bodily sensations. Your physical self responds to feelings before your cognitive self becomes aware and labels them. Further, your physical self can react to unconscious or nonconscious feelings, whereas your cognitive self can repress and deny them. Once you become more aware of experiencing these feelings, you can use more cognitive coping strategies. For example, you can take a mental step away from the situation and examine it more objectively. You have stopped just reacting and moved to examination. This can enable you to consider alternative forms of reacting and not get sucked into an emotional reaction.

STRATEGIES FOR TYPES OF DESTRUCTIVE NARCISSISM

These are suggested strategies to try based on the assumption that you will have to or want to maintain some degree of relationship with the destructive narcissist, or that leaving is not an option.

STRATEGIES FOR THE NEEDY NARCISSIST

The needy narcissists can leave you feeling drained, inadequate, and incompetent. The needs seem to be never ending. The set of strategies suggested for needy narcissists assumes that you have a need or desire to meet some of their cravings, but have come to the realization that these cravings are not capable of being satisfied. Instead of trying to guess what the person wants, ask for specifics and clarify the responses so that you have a better chance of giving what is wanted. Of course, the person would be more satisfied if you could guess what he or she wanted, but you probably have not been too successful at doing so. Do not accept hints; push for specifics. For example, if he reluctantly acknowledges that a fishing rod would be okay for a birthday gift, get a catalogue and have him point out one or two that he wants—not just what he likes, but what he wants. Examples for on-the-job specifics and clarifications would be to have the person give you written instructions, and to keep a list of your accomplishments and/or tasks readily available. Be sure to update these weekly or monthly. Then when they pile work on you or make statements that suggest you are doing less than expected, you can whip out your list and ask nicely what else is expected of you. Trying to think quickly in the grip of intense emotion, such as guilt or self-doubt, is very difficult and can lead to even more frustration.

By far, the most difficult thing to accept is that you have personal limitations and will never be able to adequately fulfill the needy narcissist's needs. Even if you were perfect, you would not be able to do so. What you can work on are your need to take care of the person, why you have this need, and your feelings of failure and self-doubt when you cannot meet the incessant cravings. These are your issues, not the other person's.

STRATEGIES FOR THE CRITICAL NARCISSIST

The critical narcissist can lead you to feeling shame, guilt, pushed away, devalued, wanting to leave, and engaging in considerable self-blame. What words trigger shame and/or guilt for you? Reflect on recent interactions that produced these feelings and identify what was done and said: these are your trigger words. Knowing your triggers can help you use some of the other strategies, showing you when to use them; this knowledge can also help prevent your emotions from intensifying or escalating.

Once you have identified your trigger words, you can stay consciously aware of when they are used and tell yourself that you do not have to have the usual response. This takes practice, but you will find your response moderating over time. Another strategy is to "go to your head" when trigger words are used. Take a cognitive step; observe what is happening to you. You do not have to let these words trigger the feelings, and by using your observing cognitive thoughts, remind yourself of this. For example, when you find yourself becoming frustrated while interacting with a critical narcissist, take a mental step back, observe yourself, and tell yourself that you do not have to be frustrated because the other person is criticizing you. This can help even when the other person is projecting blame onto you.

One difficult behavior to change is the urge to explain or defend. Most of us feel that we are being criticized or blamed because the other person does not have, or fails to understand, all the facts, and that we should give them these facts. When dealing with the destructive narcissist, particularly one who exhibits the traits of the critical narcissist, trying to explain or defend is futile. Explaining will not make a difference, and you only become more frustrated and angry when your explanation does not have a positive result or is discounted. In one sense, you have been tried, convicted, and sentenced with no chance for appeal. You will be much less frustrated and angry if you can give up these attempts to explain or defend.

Akin to all the above is the strategy of emotional insulation. This is the process used to protect yourself from the projections and identification with these. Simply put, it involves conscious awareness of your reactions when interacting with a destructive narcissist, and visualizing a wall or barrier between you and him or her. This barrier protects you from having uncomfortable feelings triggered or from projections. This strategy can be used prior to each interaction but does call for conscious effort.

STRATEGIES FOR THE DECEPTIVE NARCISSIST

The deceptive narcissists can leave you feeling exploited, questioning yourself and others, and as lacking trust. It is unfortunate that there are few options for dealing with the deceptive narcissist. Their lies, deceit, manipulation, and need to put something over on others makes it impossible to ever fully trust them, or to be sure that you are not being exploited in some way. There are times when they may be sincere, truthful, and straightforward, but you never know if or when this is the case and are much better off being somewhat wary.

You can make a habit of verifying whatever you are told by the person. This does not have to be obvious; you can be discreet when checking and cautious until you are able to verify what they have told you. For example, if you are told something is policy by your boss, whom you have identified as having many of the characteristics of the deceptive narcissist, you would want to check the policy manual or ask for a copy of the policy from someone. You may even want to ask the boss for a copy, noting that you want to become familiar with the policy so that you do not make any other mistakes.

Setting limits on your involvement with the destructive narcissist can reduce the incidences of lies, manipulation, and being tricked. Being less available makes you less of a target. However, you do run the risk of not knowing what is going on or being said, which in turn reduces your ability to combat any lies or deceptions. Setting limits on your involvement with the destructive narcissist will result in less frustration and fewer incidences of feeling like a fool or feeling exploited.

It may take a while, but it will pay off in the long run if you can accept the person as he or she is. Pointing out lies and deceptions, attempts to manipulate you and others, and unceasing efforts at putting something over is not likely to result in positive outcomes. This is counterproductive and usually produces feelings of frustration and anger in you and the destructive narcissist, neither of which solves the problem or helps the relationship. This is the way such people are; they do not see anything wrong with it and are not likely to change. Save your breath and accept that they will lie, cheat, deceive, manipulate, and trick you and everyone else.

STRATEGIES FOR THE EXHIBITIONISTIC NARCISSIST

The exhibitionistic narcissist can leave you feeling diminished, weak, incompetent, and unrecognized. Just as with the deceptive narcissist, there are few strategies for coping with the exhibitionistic narcissist that do not involve distancing yourself from them. It is not always possible to put some distance between them and you or it may not be in your best interest to do so.

The exhibitionistic narcissist is very competitive and may view every interaction as a competition they must win. There is a need to be perceived as better than everyone else, to be admired and envied, and to show off. Therefore, a coping strategy is to be noncompetitive. That is, just because the destructive narcissist is competing does not mean that you have to do so. Reduce your need to win and try to perceive interactions as collaborative rather than competitive.

This person has the capacity to produce feelings in others that they are diminished, weak, incompetent, unrecognized, and also feelings of envy.

The best strategy is to value your own competencies and not rely on the recognition of others to give them value. Making affirming statements to yourself and not letting yourself fall into identifying with the contempt shown by the exhibitionistic narcissist are two additional strategies.

DEALING WITH THE DNP IN A WORK SETTING

There are situations where your choices for coping with a destructive narcissist are reduced because of negative consequences, for example, at work. You may have a boss who has many DNP characteristics, but because his or her bosses or supervisors remain unaware of them, your boss is unlikely to be demoted, fired, or transferred. You, for whatever reason, cannot leave or transfer, putting you in a difficult position. You feel stuck, helpless, and powerless. Taking direct action and complaining to his or her boss is unlikely to be successful, and you may be perceived as a whiner, troublemaker, and so on.

Dealing with the coworker who has a DNP is as frustrating or even more frustrating than trying to deal with the boss's DNP. You encounter some of the same barriers and constraints. However, with the coworker, you have almost daily contact with him or her, and must regularly interact, thus producing more situations that are distressing to you. Some coping strategies for coping with the coworker are presented that are based on understanding the characteristics of the destructive narcissist, and how they combine and interact. These are strategies for handling disparaging comments, inappropriate credit, boasting and bragging, personal favors, giving orders, and boundaries.

COPING WITH A CO-WORKER

Disparaging Comments

You have several options for handling disparaging comments. You can ignore them, retaliate, or respond dispassionately. It is not useful to confront, attack, or agree with the comments.

The positive side of ignoring the comment is that you send a message that you do not care what the person thinks of you. The negative side is that you run the risk of others thinking that because you did not disagree or respond, you agree with the comment.

You could retaliate by pointing out to the person that he or she also has faults or makes mistakes. This action would be a clear signal that a boundary was violated. The negative outcomes could be that the person does not understand the boundary, the retaliation can be perceived as an attack by the person and other coworkers, you are perceived as defensive, and that there is some truth to the comment made by the destructive narcissist.

Responding dispassionately means you make a neutral response that carries no hint of how you really feel. Examples are a raised eyebrow, an amused smirk, saying something like, "You really think so?" with the attitude that you couldn't care less what the person thinks.

If you are open and honest with yourself, there are times when you will perceive some truth to the disparaging comment. An option would be to agree that what they have said has some merit. The positive side of that self-examination can be useful. The negative side is that the destructive narcissist then feels justified in devaluing and increases such comments. If at some point you begin to disagree or protest, the person then reminds you that you did not agree with a part or all the disparaging comment.

Inappropriate Credit

It is infuriating when others take credit for your work or ideas. It increases frustration when they do not perceive that they have done anything wrong, disagree that the work or idea was not theirs, or turn it back on you in some way. Strategies for coping include not discussing ideas with anyone you do not trust, putting your name on all your work, sending memos to the boss with your ideas, and not responding to the request from a colleague with DNP for suggestions or ideas.

When you have an idea, put it in writing to your team with a copy to the boss. Get in the habit of documenting work and ideas to the team rather than just discussing them. If there is someone you can trust, then discuss ideas with that person, but do not get into the habit of casually discussing ideas with everyone.

One habit that can be helpful is not to be too quick to respond to requests for input. For example, at a meeting if you are asked for your ideas, get into the habit of saying that you have some, but you would like to think them through or research them a little and you will get back to the group or person asking. Do get back, but do so in writing, making sure your name is attached.

Boasting and Bragging

The best coping strategy is to ignore boasting and bragging. Say nothing. If you feel you must make any response, simply grunt "Uh-huh," "Nice," or the like. Try not to listen, but do not make any negative comments.

Giving Orders

Again, the best strategy is to ignore. If you feel there is some merit in doing the ordered task, ask for it in writing. If the colleague with a DNP continues to give orders, ask the supervisor or boss for written clarification as to what your responsibilities are and see if you can get clarification on whose orders you are to follow. Confronting and/or attacking will not do any good and will most likely lead to more frustration.

Personal Favors

Neither ask for nor do any personal favors. Do not borrow or lend anything, including a paper clip.

Boundaries

You need to have firm, clear boundaries with the destructive narcissist just as you would with a child. You do not have to say anything in anger—just clearly, firmly, and consistently. For example, remind the person that such and such are your possessions, that you do not lend your possessions, that they must knock and wait for permission before entering your office or space, and that they must wait for their turn when you are talking. If it makes you feel better, you can tack on words like "I would appreciate it if you" or "Please."

COPING WITH THE BOSS WITH A DNP

The following are some possible coping strategies. The focus is on those characteristics that differ from the colleague with DNP, as many of the coping strategies used with that person can also be used with the supervisor or boss. The hardest thing to accept is that you cannot change the person. The next hardest thing to accept is the realization that the boss's own supervisors or bosses do not perceive the person as destructive, and are unlikely to receive any complaints positively, or to do anything about the troubling behaviors or attitudes. Presented are strategies to handle micromanaging, lies and misleading statements, confusing instructions, criticism, hypersensitivity, and hypercriticism.

Micromanaging

Resistance to micromanaging just prolongs the agony. You will spend more time and become more frustrated if you openly resist or protest the micromanaging. The micromanager does not understand or care that their actions result in resentment from others, are perceived as disparaging, erode self-confidence and add considerable time to the completion of any task.

The most effective coping strategy is to tolerate as much micromanaging as you can without losing confidence in your abilities. Do not take it personally because micromanaging is more a statement about your boss's unrealistic expectations for himself or herself than it is about you.

Lies and Misleading Statements

Expect that the person with a DNP will lie, make misleading statements, distort, and withhold information. Of course, the person never expects to be caught and, if confronted, will say not only that you misunderstood but that you always misunderstand. Again, confrontation is not likely to be effective.

If you can bring yourself to expect deception, then you can take preventive measures to protect yourself from the consequences of believing or acting on the inaccurate information. Preventive measures include asking for instructions in writing so that there will be no misunderstandings about the task, date due, scope or responsibility, and so on. If written documents, such as a policy manual, are available, check the information the person gave you. Build a network of people you can trust in various units so that when you are told something about which another person probably has information, you can call to verify what you were told.

Do not engage in gossip with the destructive narcissist. This person may make provocative statements about others that are lies and are calculated to get you to make a response that he or she can then carry or report to the other person. When the destructive narcissist makes a disparaging comment about someone, either say nothing, or say that this has not been your experience, and then drop the subject. Or, you can change the topic of discussion, for example, by saying, "That reminds me, I wanted to talk with you about _____."

Confusing Instructions

Coping strategies for this behavior involve some work on your part. If you are given verbal instructions, first reflect what you thought you heard back to the person and try to make sure you understood not only what was said but what the person meant by what was said. Second, write a memo detailing what you understood the instructions to be and send it to the person. Ask for a reply, noting that you want to make sure you heard correctly.

The best strategy is to avoid verbal instructions. These are usually given impromptu, on the run, in toss away statements, or in situations where it may by easy to misunderstand. You then are in the position where the supervisor or boss can say that you misunderstood and does not have to assume any responsibility for giving confusing instructions.

Criticizing

When you have a supervisor or boss with a DNP, you will probably find yourself frequently taken aback with their criticism, unwarranted charges, and attacks. Nothing is ever quite up to his or her expectations, and you are always at fault. Your boss may accuse you unfairly and leave you somewhat bewildered at what you did to cause such treatment.

Some emotional insulation will help, as will an attitude of not taking their statements personally. You may wish to unemotionally point out that the person is off target, but you would want to do it very carefully, if at all. Any opposition will generally be viewed as an attack, and it is not usually in your best interest to be perceived as attacking your boss.

You will have to develop some sensitivity to judge when it is best to ignore criticism, and when you need to pursue the issue in order to make sure the record is accurate. There are times when you must expend the time and effort necessary to make sure that the facts of the situation are clear to one and all, preferably in written form. At other times you will just want to shrug it off and go on about your work.

Hypersensitivity

Many with a DNP may be hypersensitive to perceived criticism. The initial tendency for most people is to attribute this characteristic to lack of self-confidence or low self-esteem. If the person is truly a destructive narcissist, then neither of these reasons for their hypersensitivity adequately addresses the problem. For example, if your response assumes a lack of self-confidence and you begin to make statements designed to bolster the person's confidence, you may find that it is not accepted or appreciated or that you are attacked in turn.

You may want to limit apologies to the person with a DNP. Apologies are perceived by them as an admission of guilt, which reinforces the person's attitude that you are inferior, wrong, or flawed and that he or she is superior and right. Save apologies for those times when you feel you are in the wrong and that the person deserves an apology. In short, do not get in the habit of apologizing because the destructive narcissist seems to expect an apology and you want to meet that expectation.

Hypercriticism

If nothing you, or others, do is ever right or adequate and the boss or supervisor seems to pick out unnecessary flaws, then he or she is being hypercritical. You may find your response to be redoubled efforts, resentment, or turning off. None of these do you any good, and such responses may have a negative impact. The most constructive response is to make self-affirming statements to reassure yourself that, while flawed, you do have many competencies. Still another response is to examine the criticism for validity and use it to improve if needed.

COPING WITH PARENTS WITH A DNP

As an adult, there are few effective strategies available for coping with parental destructive narcissism because the pattern for the relationship has been set and acted on for a considerable time period. You will still remain the child, no matter how old you become, and the parent will still be the parent. The parent will continue to anger, frustrate, demean, and devalue, blame, order you around, be hypersensitive to the slightest hint of criticism, expect you to show concern for him or her with little or none shown in return, unfavorably compare you with others, and so on. Your destructive narcissistic parent will not recognize your adult status or accept you as a separate, distinct individual. You may continue to try to obtain your parent's approval and acceptance, but feel doomed to failure.

The most effective coping strategy is to understand that the parent has a DNP and recognize how you have been affected by his or her behaviors and attitudes. This understanding is difficult to come by even with the help of an experienced therapist. The task involves a high level of self-exploration, commitment, and a willingness to address difficult issues. In short, the most effective coping strategy is to identify and work on your own manifestations of destructive narcissism.

Even when you are able to overcome some of the effects of the parental DNP and understand the impact on you and your adult relationships, you may still have to or want to maintain some contact or have interactions with your parents. Of course, there is always the strategy of withdrawing or severing the relationship, but other concerns, such as, the other parent, may prevent you from doing so.

If, for one reason or the other, you continue to interact with the DNP parent, even if only infrequently, you will want to use coping strategies that prevent or moderate your emotional responses of anger and frustration as well as prevent triggering feelings of shame, guilt, self-doubt, and so forth, all the old stuff with which you grew up and can easily access when interacting with him or her. Following are a few suggestions that may be helpful.

DISTANCING

As with other interactions with someone who has a DNP, you can also employ some form of distancing. Limit face-to-face interactions to a minimum. Talk with the other parent, use the telephone or e-mail and other devices in lieu of frequent direct conversation. Moving out of town may not be feasible, but moving out of the house could be. You may need to be willing to endure some deprivation that comes from a lower standard of living, but the lack of emotional wear and tear may justify doing so.

With distance, you cannot only block some uncomfortable emotions, you can better begin the process of completing separation and individuation. If you can couple distancing with significant work with a competent therapist, the process of separating and individuating will be facilitated. Although it may never be totally completed, continuing even after the parent dies, it will be significantly accelerated and more progress will be made.

REFUSAL TO ENGAGE

Identify the parental behaviors that trigger your feelings of unworthiness, self-doubt, anger, and frustration. Once you have identified what was said or done that triggered your response of one or more of these feelings, you also need to reflect on what you did or said as a response, not just what you felt. If what you did or said only served to increase or intensify the destructive narcissistic parent's behavior, such as blaming, then you can begin to develop new ways of responding that may be more effective in distracting the parent. You probably will not be able to eliminate the distressing behavior, but you may be able to moderate it somewhat.

One possible strategy is to refuse to engage in the usual interchange. Changing your response can block or truncate the interaction and thereby lessen the acceleration of the intensity of emotions stirred up in you. For example, suppose your destructive narcissistic parent always finds some way to blame you or demean you. The usual interchange is that he or she makes a charge and you deny the charge or protest. The parent then goes on to point out your many mistakes, faults, and so forth. You become increasingly angry and frustrated. Any suggestion by you that the parent is mistaken brings out another charge or tirade about lack of respect.

You could change your usual response to one that is more neutral, that is, you neither agree nor disagree with the blaming or demeaning statement, you refuse to engage. It will take considerable effort and attention not to fall into the usual pattern of interacting, but refusing to engage can be effective. Please remember that confrontation and attack are not likely to be effective with someone who has a DNP, and even less so with a DNP parent who is a destructive narcissist.

One result of refusing to engage is that the uncomfortable feelings usually generated by this kind of exchange are significantly lessened. They do not entirely go away, but you do not suffer as long as you usually would.

CHANGING YOUR EXPECTATIONS

One attitude that locks you into repeating distressing interactions with a parent with a DNP is an expectation that you can do or say something that will change the parent's behavior and attitude toward you. Since you, on an unconscious level, yearn for them to empathize, value you as a worthwhile and unique individual, appreciate you and your accomplishments, and love you, you expend considerable time and effort in this futile endeavor. These parents will only change if they are willing to spend the time and energy needed in rather long-term therapy to understand themselves and what changes are necessary. Never forget that they do not see their behaviors and attitudes as needing change.

You are not being unreasonable in expecting you parent to be empathic, not always empathic, but mostly so. It is also reasonable to expect a parent to value you as a worthwhile, unique individual. That is not to say that the parent should always agree with you or approve of your actions, but you should be able to expect that he or she will have an underlying sense of valuing you and respect for you.

Although it is not unreasonable to expect your parent to be empathic and to value and respect you, if he or she has a DNP, your parent will not do so, and you will not be able to change this. This is why the strategy of changing your expectations is suggested. If you have no expectations or certain behaviors or attitudes, then you will become less upset, angry, and frustrated when your parent does not relate to you as you are or as you wish. Realize that what you are yearning for cannot be achieved, and that realization will bring some measure of comfort.

SELF-AFFIRMING THOUGHTS

One strategy for achieving some emotional insulation is to have self-affirming thoughts available for those times when you are being devalued, blamed, criticized, or discounted in some way. Not only can you refuse to identify with the destructive statement(s), but you can also induce positive thoughts by focusing on some self-affirming statements.

Self-affirming statements are those statements about yourself that emphasize your positive points. The following list gives the stem for some self-affirming statements that you can finish by using your own descriptors. Try to list several things for each stem.

I can___(What you can do well, or your accomplishments from which you derive pleasure?)

I am (What strengths do you have that you can emphasize?)

I improved (What action or behavior is done better, or has been eliminated?

I am endearing (To whom and in what way?)

I am loveable, capable, and of worth.

INEFFECTIVE STRATEGIES

As with others who have a DNP, there are strategies that will not be effective with the parental DNP. Confronting will not produce positive outcomes, as they are more likely to exercise their parental position and accelerate their accusations, blame, and criticism. They can get and keep you on the defensive if you are so rash as to try to confront them, no matter how carefully you do it.

Fighting back or extracting some sort of revenge certainly will do nothing to promote the relationship, and you will probably end up feeling worse and alienating the other parent and siblings. Ignoring or discounting the parent will have the same effect, and although you may derive some satisfaction from these actions, the result may extract a price from you in terms of your self-perception and in other familial relationships.

COPING WITH THE SIGNIFICANT OTHER
WITH A DNP

The primary strategies are those that do not attempt to change the other person but focus on personal qualities and skills that can help. These include assuming a passive role, reflecting the grandiose self, staying engaged and interested in him or her, being accepting of the person even when he or she appears to be unreasonable, and constantly validating the person's feelings.

A Passive Role

Assuming a passive role means that you listen with understanding. Understanding that you are dealing with underdeveloped narcissism and that the other person cannot behave any differently. This can be very difficult as you visually see the person as an adult, whereas he or she is psychologically still in a more childlike state.

Reflect the Grandiose Self

The partner with a DNP may be very mirror hungry. What they present, and what others see, is the false self. The infant's true self is grandiose, and this piece is the part that the person looks to others to mirror. That is, you reflect the wonderfulness that person sees as him or herself.

Staying Engaged

Staying engaged and interested in him or her means that you attend to the person's needs. You are alert to both spoken and unspoken needs and try to meet them. Of course, it is impossible to fully meet these needs, but the degree to which you can do so allows the person to feel confident that you are interested in him or her. The other piece is that you must do so with little or no expectation that the destructive narcissist will try to meet your needs. This can be difficult to accept because, in intimate relationships, there is an expectation that there will be some reciprocity, and when there is not, relationships are negatively impacted.

BE ACCEPTING

Adopting an accepting attitude toward what may at times be unreasonable demands, expectations, blaming behavior, criticism, and so forth calls for considerable effort. This does not mean that you have to agree with what the person is saying, just that you hear him or her and do not become defensive or mount a counterattack. If done effectively, the person does not perceive you as indifferent, but as accepting that this is their perspective. With those who have a DNP you do run the risk that they think you agree with them if you are accepting, but still, this can be one of the coping strategies.

VALIDATE THEIR FEELINGS

The same process holds true for validating the destructive narcissist's feelings. When you confirm that you hear what feelings they are expressing, you are not necessarily saying that they are correct in their analyses but that they have a right to their feelings and that you respect this right.

The coping strategies discussed to this point all seem to call for a high degree of suppression of personal needs and desires. If your primary goal is to maintain the relationship at whatever cost, then you will probably be successful. But you need to be aware of the personal cost these strategies will encompass before engaging in them. Other strategies that can also be of assistance are emotional insulation, cognitive deflection, refusal to confront, and self-exploration.

Bibliography

Brown, N. *The Destructive Narcissistic Pattern*. Westport, CT: Praeger, 1998.

———. *Children of the Self-absorbed*. Oakland, CA: New Harbinger Publications, 2000.

———. *Working with the Self-absorbed*. Oakland, CA: New Harbinger Publications, 2002.

———. *Loving the Self-absorbed*. Oakland, CA: New Harbinger Publications, 2003.

Donaldson-Pressman, S. and R. Pressman. *The Narcissistic Family*. San Francisco, CA: Jossey-Bass Publishers, 1994.

Kohut, H. *The Restoration of the Self*. New York: International Universities Press, 1977.

Masterson, J. *The Emerging Self*. New York: Brunner-Mazel, 1996.

Morrison, A. (Ed.). *Essential Papers on Narcissism*. New York: New York University Press, 1986.

Index

About the Author

NINA W. BROWN is a Professor and Eminent Scholar in the Educational Leadership and Counseling Department at Old Dominion University.